T0368094

Jungle Bride

A Tale of Love and Survival in the Amazon

Vickie Foster

WESTBOW
PRESS®
A DIVISION OF THOMAS NELSON
& ZONDERVAN

WestBow Press books may be ordered through booksellers or by contacting:

WestBow Press
A Division of Thomas Nelson & Zondervan
1663 Liberty Drive
Bloomington, IN 47403
www.westbowpress.com
844-714-3454

ISBN: 979-8-3850-3940-1 (sc)
ISBN: 979-8-3850-3941-8 (hc)
ISBN: 979-8-3850-3939-5 (e)

Library of Congress Control Number: 2024925481

Print information available on the last page.

WestBow Press rev. date: 01/28/2025

Contents

Dedication and Acknowledgements

This book is affectionately dedicated to our children, Sam, Becky, and Caleb, who were companions in the sacrifices undertaken to reach the Yuquí nomads. It is equally a tribute to our faithful ministry partners, whose dedicated prayers and financial contributions were vital in making our endeavors a reality. Finally, it is a testament to my husband, Alan Foster, whose role was fundamental in creating the narrative shared within these pages. I would like to extend my heartfelt gratitude to Melanie Morgan, Judy McEachran, Brian Six, and Clint Wood for their assistance in the editing process of this book.

Preface

It's quite astonishing to reflect on the remarkable journey my life has taken. I'm not anyone exceptional, simply an ordinary American woman who has been uniquely privileged to embark on an adventure beyond my wildest dreams. My story began at the fledgling age of seventeen when I made some unexpected decisions: decisions that changed my life completely.

At the age of twenty-one, a handsome veteran missionary from Bolivia, South America walked into my life. He was no ordinary guy, but one with a fervent commitment to befriend small, hostile groups of nomads in Bolivia's Amazon rainforest. Our relationship soon blossomed into love and marriage, marking the commencement of an authentic adventure as Mrs. Alan Foster. That's when the real adventure began!

I followed this man to South America, and before I knew it, found myself in the middle of the wild Amazonian rainforest. My husband had unique skills and expertise crucial for engaging with the hostile nomads and his help was needed right away. In my narrative, I recount not only humorous incidents that unfolded as a novice missionary wife striving to keep pace with my well-seasoned husband, but also the exhilarating and hazardous experiences that come with befriending hostile jungle nomads.

The early years of my adaptation to Bolivian life presented their own set of challenges, yet they paled in comparison to the trials encountered as our decade-long venture in the jungle reached its climax. At that point, we were at the forefront of groundbreaking missionary efforts, facing pressures that were unprecedented. The weight of these challenges was daunting, but through God's grace, we found the strength to persevere. Without our unwavering commitment, and that of our co-workers, a unique group of jungle dwellers would have ceased to exist on this earth.

With the consent of my spouse, I have rephrased numerous excerpts from the concluding chapters of Alan's book *"Someone Must Die."* Throughout his book, Alan recounts the remarkable saga of how two isolated factions of hostile nomads were extended a hand of friendship by intrepid missionaries. Their intervention was critical; without it, these nomadic groups might have been annihilated by outsiders. His compelling account, titled *"Someone Must Die,"* is available on Amazon and other major vendors in both electronic and paperback formats.

Starstruck

She lay lifeless, pale and cold, in a coffin that was elegantly lined in deep burgundy velvet. Her sudden death had plunged the entire class into a state of profound shock, bereft of all the humor and infectious laughter she brought to our classroom. The details of her demise elude me... was it during my freshman or sophomore year? Even her name has faded into oblivion. Yet, the impact her death had on me still lingers. In that moment of grief, I felt confused and unsettled and the viewing upset me. I left for home and retreated to the sanctuary of my bedroom.

Despondent, I stared blankly out the window that night. The stars were especially bright, and I pondered: *Was heaven for real? Would my friend be there? Was there REALLY a supreme being living in that vast and immeasurable space beyond our galaxy?*

How can anyone wrap their mind around a God who has always existed, no beginning or end? The idea that one's life culminates in a final reckoning before a fearfully Holy God is a concept I had been taught as a child, a notion that was anything but comforting! I knew I didn't have a leg to stand on. Whoever this supreme being was appeared to be extremely remote, detached, and impersonal. Seriously! Who would even *want* to draw near to a God like that, if indeed there was a God at all!

In confusion and frustration, I yanked the curtains shut; then, turned on some bright lights and upbeat music and indulged in a good romance novel. There was more than one way to drown out those troubling reflections.

The Coffeehouse

In 1971, as I walked through the bustling streets of downtown Spokane, Washington, I had no inkling that I was about to intersect with a movement that would forever shape my destiny.

Heading for the bus stop after a morning's shopping spree, a group of young people approached me. I was taken aback to spot an old boyfriend among them. We first met the previous summer when my family rented a lake cabin, and quickly formed a mutual attraction. When the secret leaked that my new beau lived in a boy's home near the lake, I ended the relationship. I wasn't any goody two shoes back then, but I felt uneasy about dating someone with a troubled past! Yet, there he was, grinning and thrilled to see me. He introduced me to his friends, each by name, and I couldn't help but wonder where he'd acquired such good manners.

After a brief chat, he exclaimed, "Hey, I'd love to tell you about some major changes in my life since last year!" and immediately segued into talking about some sort of spiritual transformation he had experienced.

"I've met Jesus," he boldly declared. His friends affirmed him with declarations of "That's right!" "He's a different man!" and "Yeah, praise Jesus!"

This really surprised me! *Well, well, troublemaker now preaching Jesus!* Initially skeptical, I listened as his friends passionately shared their own testimonies of newfound faith. Their candid approach and infectious joy made me feel both uncomfortable and intrigued. I wondered, *Are they in some sort of cult?*

"Have you heard about the Jesus People movement?" one girl asked.

"Uh, what kind of movement?" I unwittingly responded. My question ignited a chorus of passionate responses, upon which others shared testimonies of their newfound faith. Feeling uneasy, I tried to think of a pretext to leave.

Someone jotted down a quick note and handed it to me. "There's a great coffee house we meet at regularly. Here's the address. Why not come join us this evening."

Relieved to see my bus approaching in the distance, I exclaimed, "Sorry, but there's my bus. I need to run!" and made a grand exodus. "Hope to see you at the coffee house!" someone shouted from behind.

Graduation was right around the corner and all my Senior friends were caught up with the typical end-of-year celebrations. Throughout high school, I had hung out with the crowd that loved to party and dance; but, by the end of my senior year, I began to see through the façade of youth's vanity and pride. By my last year of high school, my "soul tank" had reached empty. I was in limbo as far as any future plans were concerned.

After settling into my bus seat, I pulled the crumpled paper out of my pocket and noted the address written down. The encounter with my old boyfriend had left me intrigued and very curious. It was only 4:30 p.m., plenty of time to clean up, eat supper, and head back to town that evening. I told my mom about bumping into my old beau, his testimony, and the invite to the coffee house. She had no problem with me going.

Returning to downtown Spokane early that evening, I walked several blocks to find the place and was surprised to discover the coffee house was just a small, unobtrusive, one-story building with a large front window. Plenty of graffiti decorated the wall. *Hmmm... I'm not so sure of this.*

I peeked in the window and saw a bunch of young adults standing around inside talking. *This has to be the place. I guess I can always leave if I need to,* I reasoned and walked through the door.

Upon entering, I sensed a serene and tranquil ambience that enveloped the space with an undeniable sense of peace. The absence of loud music, dancing, drinking, and smoking that typically characterized the venues I frequented was both surprising and refreshing.

The young people wandering around spoke in soft tones; no loud boisterous voices could be heard. Most of the group looked like normal young adults in the 1970s with a few older individuals and hippie-looking characters interspersed among them. I searched for a familiar face but saw none.

Making my way to the center, I heard singing. A group of young adults stood in a circle with hands clasped and eyes closed. Swaying gently to the rhythm of their melody, they sang: "We are one in the Spirit, we are one in the Lord; ...and they'll know we are Christians by our love, by our love, and they'll know we are Christians by our love." They seemed completely oblivious to the soft-spoken din all around them.

In one corner of the large room, several were praying out loud. A hippie looking character next to me talked to another about how Jesus had completely delivered him from drug addiction. I felt completely out of place and would have left, but something about the atmosphere was very alluring and prevented me from leaving. The name "Jesus" was articulated often in the room; no rowdy voices were heard, just a warm, safe, and very inviting ambience in which Jesus was unmistakably the focus.

Five young adults approached, greeted me amiably, and invited me to join them for coffee at a table. We introduced ourselves. The ensuing conversation didn't end up being just any "Let's get to know each other" chit chat. With unified resolve, each one shared with me how their lives had completely changed since coming to know Jesus. Every one of them had their own story to tell, with an unmistakable joy written all over their faces. The ambience in that coffee house was unlike any I have ever experienced in my life.

And then one of the girls looked directly into my eyes and asked, "Do you know Jesus, Vickie?"

I was offended! I had grown up going to church, well, at least in my early childhood. I vividly remembered the life-sized figure of Jesus hanging on a cross at the front of the church, the crown of thorns on His head, the anguished and mournful eyes gazing downward, the drops of blood.

"Of course, I know who Jesus is! Doesn't everyone?" I answered assertively. "I grew up going to church."

The young lady responded carefully, "I'm not asking if you go to church or if you know who He is. I'm asking if you have ever put your faith in Him as God's Son and received Him as your own personal Savior?"

I had never been asked that question before. What was she talking about anyway?

"I'm not talking about mere head knowledge," she continued. "To know Jesus is to enter into a relationship with Him. It's impossible to have true fellowship with God until you have a relationship with His Son, Jesus Christ. God's wrath and punishment for humanity's sin was poured out on Jesus at the cross. He took the punishment for you so that you could be completely forgiven, but only if you receive God's free gift of salvation. Have you ever placed your faith in Jesus Christ as your personal Savior?"

Every one of them was so fervent and passionate about their faith that I began to feel like I was really missing out on something—something life-changing, something they all possessed—and I did not. I believed Jesus was the Son of God but not at all like they believed in Him.

"Um, well, yeah, maybe I'd like to receive Him as my Savior," I stuttered, not sure of what was required of me.

The five of them rose to their feet and encircled me. They drew in close and laid hands on my head, my shoulders, and my back. One young lady tenderly covered my hand with hers.

"Jesus, draw Vickie to Yourself," one of them prayed out loud. Another murmured, "Yes, Lord. Open her spiritual eyes that she might know You, the True and Living God." Others groaned and articulated heartfelt prayers.

Never had I heard the name Jesus used so affectionately. These young adults were in love, better yet, enraptured with Him! They talked like the Son of God was standing right there among us, like He was alive and not just hanging on a cross at the front of a church. Tears began to well up in my eyes as a deep longing welled up in my soul.

I wanted to know this "True and Living God" and have a personal relationship with Him. I wanted the intimacy they had with Jesus. *Yes Lord, please, come in and cleanse this sinful heart of mine. Make Yourself real to me,* I whispered as tears rolled down my cheeks. And with that simple but very sincere prayer, a whole new reality opened up before me and my future was changed for all eternity!

. . . .

Do you remember the Magic Eye optical illusions that were popular in the 1990s? They were colorful patterns of art that hid three-dimensional images. To see them, you had to look at the patterns in a special way. You had to hold the poster close to your eyes and stare at it until your brain perceived depth. Then, a 3-D image would pop out of the pattern like magic! Every illusion became crystal clear when you observed the poster in the right manner.

Certain books that sold these images claimed they offered "a new way of looking at the world!" This describes exactly what happened to me that night at the coffee house. I found not only a new way of looking at the world, but a completely different perception of God. A spiritual dimension and realm that I had been totally blind to suddenly became crystal clear, as if scales fell from my eyes. I invited Jesus Christ and His Holy Spirit to come in and cleanse my heart from the sin that had separated me from God and had blinded me to the Truth. That night, I became a child of God.

But as many as received Him, to them He gave the
right to become children of God, John 1:12 NKJV

My family noticed changes in my behavior right away. Swearing that had previously peppered my vocabulary was replaced with frequent assertions about Jesus. I couldn't stop talking about Him and it drove my family out of their minds! They thought I had joined a cult.

I was starving for truth, *real* Truth! I tossed the fictional romance novels, quit going to the dances and parties, and pored over God's Word with a voracious appetite. My heart spilled over with such joy; I could hardly contain it. I had found the True Lover of my soul, and He satisfied it like no one else can.

I opted not to join my twin sister one evening for a graduation party, preferring rather to hole up in my bedroom and read my Bible. My twin had had enough of all my spiritual nonsense by this time! We were graduating for goodness' sake! We should be out celebrating and having a good time, not holed up in some bedroom reading a silly Bible!

She marched right up the stairs ready to talk some sense into me. After knocking firmly, she entered my bedroom with a bold and resolute determination, but I was the one who did most of the talking that evening. Before she left my room, she too had placed her faith in Jesus and like me, had become a child of God. Others of my siblings followed suit not long after. They all knew something genuine had taken hold of me.

Often, I stepped outside at night to marvel at the stars, no longer feeling a sense of dread when contemplating an eternal and holy God. Instead, my heart overflowed with the unmistakable joy and peace of knowing I was God's beloved child. My conversion experience erased any doubt of my eternal salvation and my purpose in life. This unwavering belief has been my anchor throughout all my years.

The legacy of the Jesus People is a remarkable event in the history of American Christianity. It emerged from the counterculture of the 1960s and 1970s, when thousands of young people turned to Jesus Christ as their Lord and Savior. They embraced the gospel message of God's love, forgiveness, and salvation, and challenged mainstream culture with their radical commitment to follow the example of Jesus Christ in every area of life.

California Or Bust

Speculation ensued among family and friends about the radical change in my life, and the parents of a high school friend were especially interested to hear about my conversion. Living just a couple blocks away from us, their daughter Nancy often hung out at our house and was a good friend of mine.

Nancy was really struggling spiritually. A pastor friend of theirs, Fred Hiltz, had started up a camping program for underprivileged children in Venice, California, and needed help with supervising the youth.

Her parents had arranged for her to go to Southern California to help with the camp, hoping that Pastor Fred's influence would steer her in the right direction. When Nancy's folks heard about my newfound faith in the Lord, they eagerly invited me to join their daughter on the bus trip, hoping my influence would be good for her. The new venture sounded exciting to me, and before long, Nancy and I were bound for Venice, California on a Greyhound bus.

Venice was a vibrant beach town that boasted sun-kissed shores and a bustling two-and-a-half-mile boardwalk. Here, pedestrians wove between the ocean and the lively Bohemian, free-spirited boardwalk. When I visited the city in 1972, countless eccentric street entertainers demanded attention along the Ocean Front Walk.

Living nearby, Fred Hiltz was well acquainted with the aimless mass of humanity wandering the adjacent beach. Before his own conversion, he paid little heed to the crowds, enjoying instead the high life afforded by his lucrative job working for Walt Disney. However, once he embraced Christianity, Fred Hiltz could no longer ignore the homeless souls sleeping on the beach or the unmarried pregnant women strolling the shore, their fatherless children trailing aimlessly behind. The weight of countless young people sitting on the beach, lost in a drug-induced haze, weighed heavily on his heart. His unwavering confidence in his eternal destiny after trusting Christ ignited a powerful conviction to share the Gospel with the wandering masses. So profound was God's burden on his heart, that he left his well-paying job with Walt Disney to start a church.

Anything goes on that free spirited boardwalk; so, with guitar in hand, Pastor Fred used his captivating voice to sing and boldly proclaim the Good News: "Jesus Christ paid for your sins by dying on the cross. Salvation is a free gift to all those who believe and receive His message."

Crowds of curious onlookers drew near to listen to his preaching. Some left, disinterested in his proclamation of the Good News; however, others stayed and put their faith in the Savior. New believers began to gather in his home for Bible studies. As numbers increased, Pastor Fred built a church. His ministry expanded rapidly, and he established several homes for troubled individuals.

So dedicated was his family to reaching the lost, that they gave up the privacy of their own home to put up many who needed shelter. Nancy and I slept on inflatable mattresses in their living room while several homeless women and children filled a side room of their modest home.

Pastor Fred's son, Mark, walked through the front door one evening accompanied by a man covered with a red, blistered sunburn. The homeless man had been sleeping on the beach, and Mark invited the man to their house. "Come home with me and my dad can put you up." Their church building next door housed many homeless men during the nights while mature Christian men supervised them.

Those who lived under Pastor Fred's roof for free had to adhere to strict rules. They were required to attend both morning and evening Bible studies, as well as Sunday church services. Whether they liked it or not, they learned the Word of God, and many came to know the Lord.

They also had to contribute to household chores, such as grocery shopping, meal preparation, cleaning bathrooms and doing laundry. For many, this was the first time they felt like they had a family. I was eager to jump in with the chores and share Jesus with the women living under Pastor Fred's roof.

Fred Hiltz was a man of unwavering faith and owned two other homes at the time Nancy and I showed up. The first home was a refuge and rehabilitation center for male drug addicts. The second one cradled unwed and abused mothers, offering them a haven of safety and restoration. Competent and caring eyes watched over both homes. So profound was his ministries' impact in those days that police and social services turned to him for help when needed.

No one who served with his ministry received a salary. His staff were not driven by paychecks but by the heartfelt conviction that God's gift of salvation was free, and no sin or darkness could hide the grace He bestowed on those who sought refuge in His Son. The personnel looked heavenward for their provision and God's hand, ever generous, ensured that their ministries thrived. At that time, preparations were buzzing around me and a summer camp was awaiting underprivileged black children. What a joy it would be to see the happiness the children displayed on experiencing a camp for the first time in their lives.

One evening at Pastor Fred's church, a new chapter in my life began to unfold. I sat spellbound as Vern and Joyce Bartlett, missionaries from Brazil, spoke from the pulpit. Vern talked about their ministry while a projector hummed and revealed images of their work among jungle people living deep in the Brazilian Amazon. Like Pastor Fred, the Bartletts had forsaken their comfortable lifestyle, trading it for a higher calling: to reach isolated people groups in the remotest parts of earth with the wonderful news of the Gospel.

I was won over by their dedication and faith. *This is the essence of discipleship*, I mused. Just as the early followers left behind nets and boats, these modern-day missionaries left family, home, and occupations behind in order to follow the Lord. I believed that following Jesus was serious business and not to be taken lightly and wanted to emulate that kind of commitment.

Later that evening, I learned the Bartlett's mission organization offered a two-year, college-level Bible Institute where every book of the Scriptures was taught. It was no coincidence that the Bartletts carried applications for the Bible school that night. I had an insatiable thirst to understand God's Word in depth, from the first book of Genesis clear to the final chapter of Revelation.

Pastor Fred encouraged me to fill out an application and promised to support me $50.00 a month if I was accepted. This ended up being the only guaranteed support I had for the next three-and-a-half years in the missionary training. The tender sprouts of my faith dug deeper into God's promises as I learned to depend solely on Him. Not only was He faithful to provide for all my needs, but I had the privilege of experiencing God's faithfulness and goodness firsthand. My heart was ablaze, and I was ready to embark on a new journey with God as my guide.

And my God shall supply all your needs according to His riches in glory by Christ Jesus. Philippians 4:19 NKJV

The Promise

Upon returning home to Spokane, Washington, I eagerly filled out the application for Bible school and mailed it to Waukesha, Wisconsin, where the Institute was located. Despite misgivings due to my lack of experience with Bible schools or mission work, I was determined. Having no solid Bible teaching, no home church, and no history of involvement with Christian ministries (aside from Pastor Fred's) made me feel apprehensive. I knew I didn't seem like a very promising applicant.

Nevertheless, the desire to attend the Institute consumed me, almost to the point of being unbearable. The possibility of my application being declined disheartened me, especially since I had no home church or pastor to whom I could look for support and counsel.

At that time, my family lived just a block away from The Bethany Home, a nursing home for the elderly where I worked on a daily basis. After learning I had become a Christian, the couple overseeing the residence gifted me with my first Bible. This I read every free moment I had.

Every evening, following a day's work, I'd hasten to the mailbox, seeking any news from the Bible school, only to be met with letdown. My youthful impatience, a trait I've yet to conquer, intensified as I anticipated a reply from the Institute. A lengthy eight days passed—a whole 192 hours; 11,520 minutes—without hearing a word from the Institute. What could be the reason for their delay? Why did my longing to go to this school burn so fiercely?

I retreated to my bedroom one evening feeling pessimistic and glum and asked the Lord to encourage my doubting heart. Leafing through the Bible, I searched for any verse that would give me a glimmer of hope. *Hmmm, Leviticus, Deuteronomy, Nehemiah; not sure how to pronounce those last two.* I flipped through more pages and eventually landed in the Psalms. When my eyes lit on Psalm 37:4–5, the words leapt right off the page! I knew the Lord was speaking to me.

> *Delight yourself also in the Lord, and He shall give you the desires of your heart. Commit your way to the Lord, trust also in Him, and He shall bring it to pass. Psalm 37:4–5 NKJV*

Gazing into the night sky, I couldn't help but voice my thoughts aloud. "Is this real, God? Is this promise truly for me? You know how much joy I find in Your presence. Could it be that You would actually grant my wish to attend Bible school? Though no spoken word reached my ears, an emphatic *Trust Me and see!* resonated in my heart.

In the days that followed, I would recite Psalm 37:4–5 from an index card as I walked to my job at the Bethany Home, and review the verses again on my way back. Each evening, I eagerly checked the mailbox, only to find it empty; the silence from the Institute stretched into two long weeks. (Did I tell you how impatient I was as a youth?) I found solace in gazing at the stars from my bedroom window and whispering His promises.

> *Delight yourself also in the Lord, and He shall give you the desires of your heart. Commit your way to the Lord, trust also in Him, and He shall bring it to pass. Psalm 37:4–5 NKJV*

It didn't take long before those verses were etched deep within my heart.

About three weeks later, feeling particularly downcast one evening, I retreated to my bedroom. Gazing out at the bright stars, I poured out my heart to God. *Father, you know how badly I want to go to this Bible Institute. I'm feeling very disheartened tonight. Please, please remember your promises to me.* And just in case He had forgotten which ones I referred to, I reminded the Almighty God of the two specific promises I was clinging to (after all, there are a whopping 8,810 promises He's made in His Word). I recited the words right out loud with dramatic flair and tears streaming down my face, just to ensure they stood out on His celestial to-do list.

> *Delight yourself also in the Lord, and He shall give you the desires of your heart. Commit your way to the Lord, trust also in Him, and He shall bring it to pass. Psalm 37:4–5 NKJV*

Almost an entire month had passed. One evening, I walked to the mailbox to find an envelope lying inside that was addressed to me, Miss Vickie Starling. Realizing it was from the Bible Institute, my hands almost trembled as I picked it up. I tore open the envelope but hesitated before reading the letter, trying to prepare myself for a letdown.

All right Self, let's keep the chin up and the expectations down! Whatever their response, I need to accept it as part of God's divine plan for my life. So, brace yourself, and try not to be too disappointed, I chided myself.

I opened the envelope and began to read:

"Dear Vickie,

Greetings in the blessed name of our Lord Jesus with Psalms 37:4–5 KJV

> *Delight thyself also in the LORD; and he shall give thee the desires of thine heart. Commit thy way unto the LORD; trust also in him; and he shall bring it to pass.*

We were happy to hear from you by way of your application three weeks ago and have heard from your references also. We do want to take this opportunity to welcome you as an accepted student to begin your training here at the Bible Institute on January the 18th, 1972."

Only an intimate and loving God could have directed the writer to start with the exact Scripture promises I clung to during those weeks of doubt and uncertainty. I still have that treasured letter in my possession and God's treasured promises in my heart.

A Messy Execution

*The headless chicken strutted off into the
Richardson's dooryard, blood spouting, wings
fluttering. After a bit, it found out it was dead
and lay down decently.* Stephen King

Well, this sounds like a unique experience! I mused after the announcement was made. The following weekend, we would participate in a six-week jungle camp experience and be trained to live off the land, so to speak. The Wisconsin woods, home to many Aspen-type trees, would simulate a jungle environment where we'd be instructed in building temporary houses and living in the wilderness.

My eight female dorm mates and I agreed: learning how to survive in the wilderness sounded fun and exciting! Had I foreseen that one day I would, in fact, be living (maybe "surviving" is a better word) smack dab in the middle of the dangerous Amazon jungle, I

Vickie, left, ready for a hike

might have taken that part of the training much more seriously. At the time though, I was young, footloose, fancy-free, and ready for the adventure.

The year was 1974. By then, I had graduated from Bible School and was halfway through their Missionary Training Program and resided in the girl's dorm at the mission's facility in Fredonia, Wisconsin. It wasn't long before the staff and group of trainees, husbands, wives, and children along with seven single men and nine single women, all piled into vehicles and ventured forth into the heart of the Wisconsin wilderness. Our mission: To build rustic houses worthy of the popular TV series *100 Day Dream Home* deep in the forest. Just joking!

Armed with poles gathered from the woods, as well as twine, sheets of plastic, a heavy-duty stapler, mesh screen, and a good dose of determination, we began constructing our houses. Forget the nails and hammers! Away with the brick and mortar! This was all about the rustic vibe!

We gals tackled the building of our little jungle house with gusto. After erecting the basic frame, we set to work on our small kitchen. Twine became our secret weapon. We wove that flexible rope-like material with smooth poles to make kitchen counters and shelves. We created an oven from a barrel covered with mud which dried to a hard clay. It worked amazingly! Whether we wanted tuna casserole or hearty loaves of homemade bread, our barrel oven produced results that would even impress Martha Stewart.

No refrigerator? No problem! We dug a hole two or three feet deep in the corner of our kitchen's hard-packed dirt floor. The cavity was moistened, firmly packed down, and covered with a towel that we kept regularly dampened. Our makeshift "ice box" stayed cool enough to solidify flavored gelatin, which served as a refreshing dessert on a hot day.

Weaving a bed

Sturdy pole frames were then secured to build our three-tiered bunk beds. Twine woven between poles made for mattresses and black plastic served for the bedroom walls. One of the girls came up with the idea to cut small round windows next to each bed which were then sealed with clear plastic.

We named our cute jungle abode *The Sizzling Submarine*. Too bad we didn't have some yellow paint on hand! Clear plastic sheets were sealed to the frame to make the roof. Those transparent sheets did wonders to shield us from rain, mosquitoes, dropping twigs and nosy squirrels.

Learning to survive in some of the most remote places in the world was the name of the game, so everyone in camp had to learn to butcher a chicken. Back in 1974, we didn't have all the modern methods of getting chickens ready for the freezer, so we used the conventional manner any farmer would use back then: a hatchet and a chopping block. The experience was a first for me and thankfully the *LAST* time I ever had to butcher a chicken!

The camp was divided into groups with each team butchering fowl on different consecutive days. The morning arrived for my group, consisting of five young women from the girl's dorm and four fellas from the boy's dorm, to have our turn at the art. The guys were called on first so the gals could diligently observe how the process was done. I diverted my eyes from watching and tried to think of sugar and spice and everything nice. What a mistake!

After the boys completed their assignments smartly and efficiently, you can imagine my dismay when I was called upon to be first of the girls to try her hand. I stepped forward and a hen was placed in my arms. After stroking her red feathers and whispering my sincere apologies, I secured her pitiful little head between the large nails on  the chopping block. Next, the dreadful hatchet was placed in my hand. Deciding to get the whole ghastly procedure over as quickly as possible, I thrust the hatchet down swiftly with great resolve, but not before closing my eyes, which was another *big* mistake.

The only thing I detached from my poor feathered friend was her lovely orange beak. Cackling with hysteria, she managed to break free from the chopping block leaving an explosion of red feathers as she escaped in a frenzied run. The scene provoked a gasp of horror from my female companions and roars of laughter from the fellas. Lamentably, a staff member returned the frazzled hen with a reprimand: *"FOCUS* on what you are doing and keep your eyes *OPEN!"* Regrettably, I was given a second chance—possibly a third and fourth if needed; after all, we were there to learn!

Determined my second attempt would be my last, I focused on detaching the head from that scrawny little neck of hers, mustering all the concentration and resolve I could. With steely determination, I brought the hatchet down expeditiously and was left gaping with astonishment at a lone chicken head on the chopping block. The slaying had been accomplished.

But why was it that off to one side, I saw reddish-brown wings flapping hysterically? I turned to see my headless hen unconsciously running and casting herself about, all the while splattering blood everywhere. The young women shrieked with disgust. The fellas howled with delight. The poor red hen couldn't even cackle without a head but continued to throw herself about.

Full of astonishment, I questioned: Had I not killed her? Much later I read an article about a headless rooster in Colorado that had lived for eighteen months without a head! He was dubbed Miracle Mike. Was this little red hen to become a Miracle Maisy!?

Truthfully, she hadn't thrown herself about for more than sixty seconds, but to this executioner, it seemed more like sixty minutes. One staff member remarked that she, indeed, had run around headless longer than any of the other chickens. No doubt, the initial beak removal process had revved her shattered nerves to overkill.

I breathed out a huge sigh of relief, thankful the whole disgusting procedure was over, at least for the most part. We were then ushered into an area to learn how to defeather our warm-blooded fowl, remove the innards, and cut the poultry into pieces for cooking. The evening promised a bounty of chicken to be breaded and deep fried, yet somehow the enthusiasm for crispy fried chicken had flown the coop among the gals in the dorm.

The Trainee Meets the Veteran

I first met the handsome, jungle-forged man who would later become my husband during the last phase of my three-and-a-half-year missionary training course located on the beautiful Lake of the Ozarks in Camdenton, Missouri. In that lovely location, the students delved into specialized training: cross-cultural church planting, phonetics, language methodologies, and cultural studies.

But the preparation there had an unexpected twist for me: a six-week crash course in medical skills. From administering injections to assisting in childbirth, we covered it all. The graphic nature of a real birthing process shown in a film depicting midwifery nearly caused me to faint. I never thought I'd need to help with childbirth; yet, as fate would have it, God had other plans. When serving in a remote corner of the world, the basic medical training we received became a lifeline.

Alan communicating from a jungle beach

Around this time, a new face appeared at the Language School as a temporary addition to the staff. I resided with Beverly Foster, along with nine other single women in the girls' dorm, where Beverly informed me the new staff member happened to be her brother Alan. He had recently arrived from Bolivia. Being close friends, she confided in me that he wasn't there just to help the training program; he was hoping to find a wife. As she related his backstory to me, I was intrigued. After spending four intense years deep in the heart of the Amazon jungle, working with hostile nomads, he longed for companionship. *Poor chap!* I thought, *Of course he needs a companion!* I promised Beverly I would be faithful to pray that God would provide him a wife, never *ever* imagining I might be the answer to my own prayers!

Alan, along with his two sisters, Beverly and Anna, was no stranger to rugged living. As missionary kids raised in Bolivia, South America, they understood firsthand the challenges of primitive jungle conditions. Their parents, Les and Lois Foster, had courageously befriended a treacherous group of Yuquí nomads. Alan drew heavily upon the methods he had learned earlier at the Language School while working alongside this unique people group. Having firsthand experience applying the techniques helped him greatly in assisting others who were learning those methodologies. Being fluent in Spanish and Yuquí was an added plus as he coached students heading to Latin America.

It wasn't long before Beverly's brother arrived at one of our singles' gatherings with a girlfriend he'd met at church. I was happy for him and hoped their love would flourish. But life has its twists. The girl, perhaps daunted by the weight of missionary commitment, stepped away, leaving Alan adrift once again.

Undeterred, her brother recalibrated. He decided to focus on the single girls who had already pledged themselves to the missionary path and asked his sister to suggest several possibilities. There were others, of course—eleven single girls in that dorm—but, unbeknownst to me, she urged him to start with none other than yours truly.

Alan, resolute and purposeful, embarked on his quest to get to know this Vickie Starling. Until then, he'd been a shadow, a silhouette against the backdrop of our missionary training. But suddenly, there he was, greeting me by name and walking me back to the dorm after classes. His intentions were obvious: He wanted to get to know me.

With dark hair and a complexion that seriously flattered his distinct flair with the Latin culture, I admit I was attracted. Not only was he nice looking but serious natured and polite. This young veteran missionary walked to a different beat from the other American guys I had dated. This attracted me. Nevertheless, I was new to my Christian faith and wanted to be certain that God approved of any relationship I had with a guy. So, at another singles' party one weekend, in my overzealous caution, I purposely avoided him. Whenever he came near me, I turned away and talked to other guys who were just friends. I would have rather talked to Alan, but I didn't want to rush things. After an hour or so of chit-chatting with a couple of guys, I left. Bleh! I wasn't enjoying the party anyway.

Moseying back to the dorm that night, I kicked at the rocks and pebbles under my feet and felt like I should be kicking myself. No doubt, the young missionary had read my aloofness as the cold shoulder, and I had nipped a relationship with him before it even had time to bud.

With a gloomy heart, I looked up to the bright stars, and prayed, *Lord, if You are behind this, you know I sure messed things up tonight! If this is of You, would you give me another chance?* I didn't feel too optimistic after giving Beverly's brother the cold shoulder all evening, but managed to leave it in God's hands.

Arriving back at my dark, empty dorm, I turned on the light. No sooner had I hung up my jacket than the phone rang.

"Hello," I answered.

"Hello, is this Vickie?"

My heart skipped a beat. It was Alan's voice. "Yes, it is." I responded.

"I was wondering if you would like to join me in seeing the Ozark Opry tomorrow night." No meaningless small talk or beating around the bush! (Had I mentioned that once his course was determined, Alan moved with resolve?) My inattentiveness at the party hadn't deterred him one whit.

I was happy to say "yes" and whispered a heartfelt "Thank you" heavenward. We thoroughly enjoyed ourselves at the Ozark Opry the following night. After that, we started dating, writing letters when we were apart, and falling in love. Six months was plenty of time for Alan to dismiss any doubts about marriage; after all, he was twenty-seven and had a missionary career to get back to. One night, after walking around the gorgeous Lake of the Ozarks, he popped the question.

I was well acquainted with the many photographs and stories of the hostile nomads by then; still, his proposal caught me totally off guard. Not only would I be saying yes to becoming his wife, but yes to his missionary call as well. There was no doubt that I loved him; nevertheless, I hesitated a few seconds knowing this was a very solemn commitment. Within those fleeting seconds of hesitation, I realized I just couldn't live without him. "Yes, I will marry you," I responded.

The lake shimmered with the moon's golden light as we kissed for the first time. We agreed on a date to pick out rings and then he walked me back to the dorm. Before I went inside, he gave me a wrapped box. "This is it until we pick out a ring," he said with a smile. "Hope you enjoy chocolates!"

I heard a loud commotion coming from the kitchen as soon as I entered the dorm. One of my dorm mates became engaged that very same evening and was excitedly sharing the proposal story with the other gals. After offering her congratulations and a heartfelt embrace, I quietly retreated to my own space.

Meanwhile, I clutched the unwrapped box of chocolates and my trusty Bible (because chocolate and Scripture go together like crackers and cheese) and settled into a cozy chair in the living room. The dorm buzzed with excitement. My roommate's engagement had triggered a cheerleading squad of giggles, but I wasn't ready to spill my secret just yet.

I sat in the comfy chair, unwrapping chocolates. Each foil revealed a sweet surprise: caramel, hazelnut, and coconut that tasted suspiciously like a tropical vacation.

As I popped a truffle into my mouth, butterflies jitterbugged in my stomach, doing the cha-cha with my nerves.

You'll be heading to the Amazon jungle, I mused, giving myself another reality check. *Am I really cut out for such an adventure?* With my nerves still doing the jitterbug, I popped another chocolate into my mouth and silently prayed: *Lord, I can't imagine life without Alan, but seriously! The jungle?* I chewed on yet another dark chocolate truffle hoping the serotonin would begin to do its magic. Knowing I hadn't made any short-term commitment, I prayed: *Lord, did I make the right choice?* Needing a reassuring word from God, I opened my Bible to where I had been reading in 1 John, chapter four. I read until my eyes lit upon verse 18.

> *There is no fear in love, but perfect love*
> *casts out fear. 1 John 4:18 NKJV*

Fear: That was my problem! Fear of the unknown had cast shadows on the joy I should have been experiencing after saying "yes" to the one I loved so dearly.

As I reflected on God's words to me, peace began to flood my heart and all my apprehensions and fears dissipated. I reveled in the calm. Then, armed with a good dose of serotonin and a heart spilling over with God's peace, I marched off to bed. I would announce my engagement to the girls the following morning.

Vickie and Alan

Not long after, Alan and I, along with a friend, drove to Spokane, Washington, where he would meet my parents and family for the first time before we planned our wedding. Alan wanted my parents to know what their daughter would face after she left the U.S.A., so he showed them many pictures and slides of the Yuquí. My folks were drawn to him right away and could see that I was in good hands.

Nonetheless, hearing stories and seeing pictures of the Yuquí is nothing compared to actually living among those unique nomads! The true magnitude of my decision did not really hit home until I was smack dab in the middle of the isolated Amazon jungle by my husband's side.

★★★★★★★

The Nomads

Then I heard the voice of the Lord saying, "Whom shall I send? And who will go for us?" And I said, "Here I am. Send me! Isaiah 6:8 NIV

They proudly called themselves Mbia, a word meaning "the people". Presently, they are known as the Yuquí (you-KEY). Before missionary intervention, these fierce nomads roamed the jungle, believing they were the only human beings on the face of the earth.

Yuquí departing on an overnight trip

Armed with a 7–8-foot bow and arrows, and long bushy black hair, the Yuquí men were truly impressive warriors. Possessing unparalleled prowess in drawing back the bark rope strings of their massive palm wood bows, they had the capability to hunt and fell large prey weighing between 500–600 pounds. The sharp curved points of their bamboo-tipped bleeder arrows, measuring twelve to fifteen inches long and two inches wide, ensured that their prey would bleed to death.

Roughneck repairing arrows

The Bolivian government wasn't even aware the nomads occupied the jungle until the early 1950s. At that time, they considered that part of the rainforest as "vacant land" and granted the property to major lumber concessions and unemployed miners for farming. As nationals started settling into what the jungle nomads believed was their own land, killings and fighting ensued. The *Mbia* believed these *abaa* (outsiders) were really reincarnated "spirits" of their deceased kin intent on harming them.

Historically, the Yuquí people lived in relative isolation until sustained contact with our missionaries began in the mid-1960s. At that time, there were about fifty Yuquí in the first band the missionaries befriended. Through missionary endeavors, the Yuquí population increased to roughly 130 by the 1990s. Initially, outsiders believed the nomads were part of the Sirionó people. However, further contact revealed that the Yuquí were a distinct and very unique ethnic group.

Yuquí warriors with jungle fruit

The *Mbia* faced many challenges when the colonists began clearing the land in preparation for farming. When the jungle nomads stole crops and goods from the encroaching farmers, the farmers retaliated with gunfire. Angered by the colonists' intrusions into what they considered their homeland, the Yuquí killed a colonist and burned down his thatch-roofed house while wounding others. Things really escalated from there.

In retaliation, the settlers sent out hunting parties to search for the nomads. When they encountered a Yuquí encampment in the jungle and discovered most of the men were gone hunting, they surrounded the nomads' camp and opened fire with their rifles until all the *Bia* were either killed or had fled. Four Yuquí children were captured in one incident.

The enraged warriors then took revenge by piercing the backs of unsuspecting Bolivians with their spear-sized arrows. The escalating crisis became so severe that the Bolivian government planned on sending in the military to completely annihilate the "savages" once and for all. God had other plans though for this small and unique people group.

Around that time, Alan's parents arrived in Bolivia and worked alongside other missionaries in the jungle town nearest to where the nomads roamed. Soon these missionaries found themselves right in the middle of the escalating crisis. When the missionaries offered to attempt making friends with the hostiles and help them settle down, the government was glad to let the missionaries try befriending the warriors.

Anthropologists who later studied the nomad's culture deemed the Yuquí to be one of the least culturally developed people groups in the world. Throughout their nomadic travels, they roamed naked and never established permanent homes. During

Early contact with nomadic Yuquí

cold, wet tempests that lashed the rainforest, they sought refuge under makeshift palm leaf shelters. Their crude sanctuaries did little to protect them from the heavy downpours.

Fire was critical for the *Mbia*'s survival. None of them have any recollection of ever being without it. They continually carried fire with them, smoldering embers to ignite new fires when they camped for the night. Without that source of heat, they couldn't keep warm when temperatures dropped to the 50s during the cold, rainy season. Without fire, they couldn't roast the game they shot in the woods.

I vividly remember the jungle's chill penetrating clear to my bones during those frigid wet months in the Amazon. Cold fronts called *surazos* blew in from the south pole and often brought violent rainstorms with them. Temperatures of 90°F or more would plummet to the low 50s in a few hours' span. Our rustic missionary houses built from split palm boards couldn't keep out the damp cold, so we wore heavy sweaters and jackets. The nomads suffered much during those storms, often huddling under palm leaf shelters as they desperately tried to keep their smoldering embers from being extinguished. Sometimes, *surazos* lasted for weeks, with the sun rarely peeking through the dark clouds. During these times, I often thought about what some people in the U. S. said before we left for the mission field: "Leave them alone! They're happy as they are." It was a foolish statement by those living in comfort and luxury!

Typical Yuquí camp

The gravity of the Yuquís' condition almost overwhelmed me during those long stormy spells. As I gazed out on the drenched, dark jungle beyond our clearing, my mood would turn as gray and heavy as the atmosphere. I knew God had commissioned us to this assignment, but the monumental difficulties in reaching these primitive nomads with the Gospel seemed especially hopeless during those cold wet tempests. I had to remind myself that God was the one who had appointed us to the job and He was the one who would finish it. It was His constraining love for the nomads, coupled with His enabling power, that helped us persevere when things seemed impossible.

The successive days of pouring rain limited the amount of hunting the nomads could do, and game became scarce. Finding meat was a driving force for them. Without it, the warriors and their families went hungry. Making fires during these heavy

Father and son

rains was extremely challenging and it was all they could do to keep the smoldering embers from being snuffed out. The Yuquí often chanted during the tempests, eerie chants made to pacify the spirits of their dead. After all, they believed the angry spirits were causing the miserable storms.

Once the *surazos* blew over, the nomads resumed their travels as they hunted and made temporary camps throughout their never-ending wanderings. Slaves did most of the dirty work among these bands, having been born into the caste system from the bloodline of their ancestors. Yuquí slaves faced some of the most pitiful lives ever to be imagined.

They were the work horses, often hauling heavy and bloody game back to their camp after hunting trips and climbing thorn-infested trees to retrieve honey from a beehive. Yuquí slaves kept the fires going all night to repel mosquitoes with the smoke so their masters wouldn't be harassed as they slept in their crude hammocks.

Life was cheap to the Yuquí, and death came frequently. If a high-class nomad died, their slave might be killed to accompany the dead person's spirit in the afterlife in order to appease his or her spirit. If it was a chief who died, as many as four or five slaves could be killed. Needless to say, this didn't help increase their dwindling population, and the number of the first band of Yuquí was reduced to just four dozen people by the time my husband's parents and co-workers were able to befriend them. My husband's book, *"Someone Must Die,"* details many of the unnerving situations the

Yuquí young people at home at Biá Recuaté

missionaries faced in their attempts to befriend the first group before it was too late.

After years of daunting challenges, the first band of Yuquí was finally be-friended, completely won over by the missionaries' unwavering dedication and patient demonstrations of love. The *Mbia*, now referred to as the *Bia*, decided to settle down at the missionary base on the Chimoré River. This site today is officially recognized as Biá Recuaté (the people's land) and has been established by the Bolivian government as the private property of the Yuquí people. Thanks to

proper training in husbandry and hygiene, along with the medical care provided by the missionaries, the Yuquí numbers have more than tripled. Having changed from rugged nomads struggling to survive the unforgiving jungle, the Yuquí people have joyfully embraced a new way of life.

Current Yuquí community

First Impressions

Go from your country, your people and your father's household to the land I will show you. Genesis 12:1 NIV

The window seat offered unfettered views of the Andes' jagged, desolate peaks as we soared over the highlands of Bolivia. Our destination was Cochabamba, a principal city nestled in a fertile valley, 8,430-feet up in the Andes Mountain range. There I would meet Alan's parents and his older sister for the first time.

Alan had a deep affection for the people and culture of this country. Having grown up there, he was returning to his roots, the place of his upbringing. He was not only accustomed to life in Cochabamba but was well acquainted with surviving the untamed jungles of Bolivia. His family, fluent in Spanish, felt at home with the people in both the highlands and the lowlands. I, on the other hand, was a complete novice, having left my family, home, and everything familiar to be by my husband's side in this foreign land. Upon our arrival in Cochabamba, we were warmly welcomed by Alan's parents and sister Anna.

Cathedral in Cochabamba

His family delighted in guiding me around Cochabamba, fondly known as "The Garden City." I marveled at the flowers, fountains, and lovely plazas. We enjoyed visiting an old cathedral on the main square where the city was a vibrant blend of age-old traditions sparked with new energy.

The quaint descendants of the Aymara or Quechua ethnic people, wearing traditional home-spun woolen apparel and sandals created from old car tires, strolled the same sidewalks as young adults sporting the latest styles. Dusty hills on the outskirts of the metropolis were crammed with lowly adobe houses while pricey modern homes abounded near the city. It seemed Cochabamba was indeed a city of contrasts!

Street scene in Cochabamba

Indigenous women, known as *cholas*, from the Andean highlands were a common presence. These women, with their distinctive and colorful attire, are a symbol of the rich cultural tapestry of the highlands of Bolivia. Donning ankle-length multi-layered skirts of turquoise, purple, pink, etc., their clothing embellished the typically blue sunny skies of Cochabamba. Multiple layers of underskirts gave their skirts a distinct puff enhancing the charm of their swaying hips as they sauntered the streets. Adorned with long black braids and donning top hats and vibrant shawls, the *cholas* often captivated newcomers who were eager to capture a picture. However, photographers taking pictures without proper consent, might find themselves evading a tire sandal hurled their way.

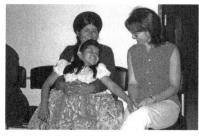
Vickie with Bolivian friends

The heart of the city bustled with motion and activity. Bicyclists and motorcyclists zigzagged between automobiles as vehicles honked at the intersections, the loudest and most determined claiming the right of way. Buses filled to capacity droned by with passengers hanging out the door. It was with some relief we returned to the outskirts of the city where the mission guest home was located. There the hustle and bustle were much more low-key.

Intrigued by a variety of unfamiliar noises, I set out one morning to investigate the local area. As I wandered through the adjacent *plazuelas* (little plazas), I came upon the origin of the strange cries that reached my ears every day. It turned out that *cholas* were marketing their products in a quirky sing-song fashion by crying out in high pitched nasally voices to promote their goods: *pasteles* (delicious fried cheese turnovers), *jugo de naranja* (freshly squeezed orange juice), *api* (a colorful, sweet breakfast drink made from purple and white maize with cinnamon) as well as *pancitos* (hearty cheese covered buns freshly baked in clay ovens).

On weekends, the air outside of the mission compound was filled with resounding clangs. It soon became clear that these noises were the result of metal garbage lids being struck together, a makeshift signal to inform the local residents that the garbage collection was about to begin.

One Saturday, I exited the back side of our compound onto a side street just as a garbage truck roared by, leaving a small, elderly peasant lady tottering far behind. She scurried as fast as her short little legs could carry her with a garbage bag swinging forcefully in her hand. With a shrill, feeble voice, she hollered at the driver with all her might. Her face was a stormy mix of adorable and about to explode, and I suspected her cries were peppered with expletives aimed at the oblivious trash collectors.

I worried she'd take a tumble on the brick paved street, so I dashed out the door like a heroine, snatched up her trash bag and raced towards the truck, arm flailing to catch the driver's eye. My efforts paid off as he halted, allowing me to swiftly toss the refuse into the back of the garbage truck.

A few minutes later, the breathless little lady approached me, grabbed my arm affectionately, and gave me one of the sweetest toothless smiles I'd ever seen, her eyes beaming up at me. She didn't reach much past my waist in height. She articulated some unintelligible words in Quechua or Aymara or whatever language she spoke, which I interpreted as a hearty "Thank you my dear."

Mamita

Over the years, this dear lady and I became good friends. I affectionately called her Mamita, a term of endearment. We couldn't understand each other's language; she didn't speak a word of English, and my basic Spanish was lost on her, but love transcends language barriers. Spanish is the principal language in Bolivia, but with 36 Indigenous languages recognized, communication in the country can be quite challenging.

During my respites from the jungle, I always seized the opportunity to bring Mamita fresh produce and flowers from the Saturday market, anything to cheer her bleak, one room adobe house. Her warm embrace and toothless smile were all the reward I ever needed.

Just across the street from her tiny adobe hut stood a grand and stately white mansion encircled by a decorative iron fence with a majestic fountain at the heart of its well-manicured grounds. Mamita's dingy, one-room hut paled miserably against the grandeur of that luxurious house. Yes, Cochabamba was definitely a city of

Mamita's adobe home

contrasts! My heart yearned to share the Gospel with Mamita and convey the depth of Jesus's love for her. At times, I'd converse with her in basic Spanish, envelop her in a warm hug, and gesture heavenward while repeating the name Jesus, hoping to communicate God's love for her.

One day I was ushered into a popular Bolivian restaurant on the bustling main square by my husband and Fernando, a national friend of his. With a nudge from my adventurous spouse, I decided to sample the local cuisine and ordered *Picante Mixto*: a hearty ensemble of meats drenched in a savory picante sauce, accompanied by rice and potatoes. The beef cow tongue, however, was a delicacy I wasn't quite prepared for, so I stealthily transferred it onto Alan's plate (a tactic I often resorted to back then) and eagerly dug into the chicken, which was delicious. Meanwhile, Alan and Fernando were lost in a sea of nostalgia, conversing in Spanish which mostly eluded me.

Pleased with the chicken, I proceeded to the rabbit, having heard it tasted much like poultry. True enough, the initial bites were succulent and delightful. Yet, as I navigated through the boney piece for the remaining scraps of meat, the two men remained deep in conversation, hardly taking notice of their meals. In pursuit of more flavorsome morsels, I flipped the boney piece of rabbit over, only to be met with an extremely unnerving sight: a head with two beady eyes stared at me through the red picante sauce. The display on my plate was shocking!

Stifling a gasp of disgust behind my napkin, I stared at the cuisine with astonishment. The head displayed a sinister grin with two pointed incisors. Two small ears perched atop its' well-defined snout, all of it bathed in the rich, red savory sauce. I was stunned. I was appalled. I was utterly lost for words!

Alan's friend, Fernando, noticed my distress and quickly started to apologize. He then clarified that in Bolivian dining, rabbit is often replaced with guinea pig, a delicacy once reserved for nobility and still consumed entirely, head to toe, to this day. Perhaps I should have felt honored to be offered a dish once enjoyed by royalty? Thus began my introduction to typical Bolivian cuisine, which, regardless of the guinea pig head, really is *very* delicious.

Those initial weeks in Cochabamba were spent diligently immersing myself in language study and learning the local culture. However, just as I was getting the hang of things, my Spanish lessons came to an abrupt halt. Missionaries working at the Chimoré jungle base needed our help with a semi-civilized group of Yuquí; well, truthfully, they needed Alan's help since he was the one with all the experience and language. I was just his greenhorn bride tagging along behind trying to learn the ropes. Thoroughly disappointed to hear my language lessons were to be put on the back burner and having to bid adieu to the beautiful "Garden City," I dutifully packed my bags.

Thus, I was thrust into the harsh reality of jungle life much sooner than I expected being married to this veteran missionary man of mine. Alan's expertise with the nomads was always in great demand, both with the semi-civilized group at the Chimoré base as well as with hostile groups the missionaries were trying to befriend. So, buckle your seat belt, and join me on my first Cessna airplane ride into the Amazon Rainforest.

The Primeval Forest

If you want to keep alive in the jungle,
you must live as the jungle does.
John Wyndham

Staring out the window in rapt fascination, I was struck with the sheer magnitude of the rainforest. The jungle's canopy looked like an endless expanse of dense, green broccoli florets. In truth, what looked like endless patches of broccoli were really lofty, emerald crowns of giant jungle trees that

The Amazon rainforest

soared over a hundred feet and more skyward. Slivers of brown rivers twisted and curled their way through the pristine green wilderness below like snakes. These were tributaries of the mighty Amazon River.

We left Cochabamba that morning flying in a single engine Cessna aircraft. This was my first experience flying in a small plane. Our missionary pilots are well trained, and it didn't take long for me to relax in the back seat and enjoy the scenery. The pilot not only had years of experience navigating over the high Andes Mountains but

Landing on a jungle airstrip

was an expert at landing and taking off on short jungle airstrips.

Our destination was the Chimoré missionary base. It was at this location that Alan's parents and co-workers had befriended the first band of Yuquí. Back then, these

Yuquí were a treacherous and hostile group of nomads. However, by the time we arrived as a couple, this group of Yuquí were beginning to settle down at the base.

In due course, the pilot pointed to a tiny dot far off in the distance. "There's the Chimoré base," he hollered over the roar of the engine. After reducing speed, he began to descend. Lush greenery from towering trees enveloped our sight as we descended, revealing a grassy runway nestled below. We descended gently, soaring right above the landing strip. Suddenly, an abrupt and powerful thud signaled our touchdown, after which we taxied down the strip until we came to a complete stop.

We were stepping in for Ed and Jane Wiebe, missionaries overseeing the Chimoré base, who were long overdue for a break. Their colleagues, Bob and Mary Garland, were on leave in the U.S., leaving only one other missionary for support, making their tasks very demanding. We were to cover their responsibilities for a month. The Wiebes were set to leave for Cochabamba on the same Cessna we arrived in, with their flight scheduled in just a few hours. This gave Alan and me minimal time to learn the ropes.

From a distance, I saw a group of brown-skinned Yuquí natives huddled next to the airstrip alongside the Wiebes. They were eagerly waiting for our arrival. When the spinning propeller ground to a complete halt, the engine was shut down, and the pilot swung the door wide open.

Eager to greet us

A jolt of heat and humidity blasted me as I stepped out of the plane. I felt like I had just stepped into a sauna. Alan, next to me soaking it up, exclaimed heartily, "Ahh, can you feel the humidity? I just LOVE it!" Well, this new bride of his certainly did not share in his enthusiasm. Being raised in the crisp, rejuvenating air of the Rocky Mountains, I found the heat and humidity oppressive. Not only did I not "just love it" then, but I don't "just love it" now, nor did I ever learn to "just love" the jungle's muggy heat the entire ten years I lived there.

Exiting the plane

The stifling air was thick with a noticeable scent: a cocktail of fresh plant life intermingled with the musty decay of the rainforest floor. It wasn't unpleasant, just very distinct, and lingers in my memory to this day. Continuous hums, thrums, whistles and buzzing declared the lively presence of unseen creatures in the woods and around us. That soundscape was quickly drowned out by the animated gibberish of the Yuquí who rushed over to embrace us. And just like that, I found myself whisked away into a completely different realm.

We all stood huddled together in our tropical steam bath; their hands stroked our heads and arms affectionately. Alan playfully teased them in their native tongue, and they responded with hearty laughs and animated exclamations, giving the back of their heads

Yuquí friends

a playful smack in typical Yuquí fashion to show their amusement and joy. While their faces gleamed with delight, mine gleamed ever brighter with perspiration. The Yuquí adored my husband and were overjoyed to see he had arrived with his new bride.

We made our way to our jungle lodgings with Yuquí surrounding us. The crowd tagged along in front, behind, and at our sides. The younger ones held our arms tightly, giggling and gazing devotedly into our faces. *This must be how the Beatles felt when they hit the States,* I mused.

After arriving at our temporary jungle home, we hauled our luggage and boxes inside. Cheerful faces peered through the screened kitchen window from the outside porch. Privacy, I learned, would not be a luxury I'd often enjoy in my new environment. Looking at the overly affectionate crowd of devotees made it hard for me to even imagine them as they were thirteen years previously: fierce, naked nomads renowned for killing outsiders with their seven-foot bleeder-tipped arrows.

By the time I arrived, these Yuquí had decided to settle at the Chimoré base where they found safety, shelter, and ample food. During their nomadic years, the Yuquí struggled with catching fish, nor could they swim. Alan introduced net weaving to them which enhanced their catch significantly. It wasn't uncommon for them to lug fish over twenty-five pounds past our jungle house as they made their way back to their camp. The gnawing hunger they faced as nomads diminished once they started learning skills in agriculture

Yuquí with arrows and fish

and animal husbandry. Their health improved drastically with the medical care missionaries offered. The Yuquí gained knowledge about cleanliness and good hygiene, were treated for parasites and snake bites, and the women were assisted in childbirth by the missionary wives, reducing the high infant mortality rate significantly.

Assisting a Yuquí woman giving birth was definitely something I never expected to do! I was a newbie at everything and hadn't even experienced pregnancy yet. Seriously! Who in the world would even think of thrusting a novice like me into midwifery right after landing in a foreign country? Well, apparently God did!

I was still trying to navigate the ropes of being a missionary wife and juggling two new languages in two wildly different cultures (Spanish and Yuquí) when *bam!* I found myself smack dab in the middle of the jungle receiving a three-hour crash course in medical duties. And just like that, voila! I emerged as camp nurse and midwife before I even knew how to say *"Push!"* in the Yuquí language! What on earth was God thinking? I didn't have time to ponder that mystery. Jane Wiebe was leaving in a few hours and needed to cram in a quick tutorial on clinic operations. So, slap on that nurse's cap and join me for some on-the-job training!

The Half Doctor

A half doctor near is better than a whole one far away.
German Proverb

"As you know, the Yuquí camp is across the river from us so, it just makes sense to keep her close by. She's about seven months along and is staying in the old bamboo shed not far from the house," Jane Wiebe was saying.

"She'll probably be just fine till I return, but just to be safe, here's a little black box with instructions and everything you need if the baby should come early. Keep it at the house and become familiar with all the delivery procedures."

Waiting for store to open

Hmm, hadn't I read a quote somewhere? "Panic plays no part in the training of a nurse." *There's no need to panic; she's just taking precautions,* I chided myself.

"I'm calling the *Bia* by their Spanish names to make it easy for you," Jane continued. "Juan had a mishap with a machete a few days ago. The butterfly stitches have held up fine, but you'll need to keep an eye on the wound and change his bandage every couple of days. Everything you need can be found inside this cupboard." She opened the cabinet and went over the contents inside.

While Jane was the seasoned nurse on base with plenty of experience, my training was limited to the six-week medical course I went through at the Language Institute, you know, the one with the childbirth film that nearly caused me to pass out. Jane and Ed were set to depart in the same Cessna plane we arrived in, so with only a few hours left, we got down to business.

"Here's the kettle of needles and syringes that need to be sterilized," Jane went on. "You need to boil the used ones every night for half an hour. Then, let them drip-dry. My apologies, but disposable needles are a no-show in the jungle, so brace yourself for some less-than-sharp pokes with the older needles."

"It's probably been a while since you've given a shot," Jane remarked. "Here, practice a few times on this orange." She handed me the supple, ripe citrus with a syringe and needle. I filled the syringe with water, inserted the needle, and with the precision of a newbie, jabbed it into the thick rind and administered the injection.

"Not bad! But remember to grasp the flesh firmly between your thumb and forefinger and aim the needle at a sharper angle." Jane instructed. "Remember: A swift motion of the wrist is the key. The faster it goes in, the less it hurts."

I kept at it. "You're doing great!" Jane exclaimed looking over my shoulder and giving me a reassuring smile. "Stay confident and act like you know what you're doing. You'll soon be giving shots like a pro!"

The brief span we had to review medical duties left my mind reeling. I planned to practice administering injections again that evening knowing I'd be on my own in the morning. There certainly wasn't a lack of citrus fruit to practice on.

The hours passed quickly and before long, Ed and Jane were bidding adieu and boarding the plane. With safety measures in place, the pilot fired up the engine. After a few gut-wrenching squeaks and rattles, the steady, robust whir of the blades ensued, creating a refreshing gust of wind that tousled our hair and cooled our perspiring brows.

The red and white Cessna taxied to the end of the runway and turned around. Then, in full throttle, the plane roared down the airstrip before lifting off into a cloudless, blue sky. We caught glimpses of our co-workers waving their goodbyes as they soared past. We returned the gesture. The plane shrank in size until it finally disappeared into the blue yonder; the whine of the engine echoed through the jungle trees and grew softer and softer with each passing moment. Then there was silence.

I don't know if it was the lonely drone of the engine fading away or the realization that we were so far from civilization, but their departure hit me like a heavy, wet blanket of abandonment. Jane and I only spent a few hours together, but already I longed for her practical advice and company. There I was, a newbie missionary spouse with a big responsibility ahead of me and no other missionary gal in sight. Sure, my jungle-seasoned hubby was there, and Dick Strickler, our faithful solo coworker, knew his stuff. Plus, we had our HF (high-frequency) radio to communicate with doctors in Cochabamba if an emergency came up, but still: *If only another American missionary lady were here,* I mused, *it would be nice to have some female companionship.*

Unexpectedly, a promise from God emerged in my mind:

> *Fear not, for I am with you; do not be dismayed, for I am your God. I will strengthen you and assist you; I will support you with My righteous right hand. Isaiah 41:10 ESV*

Dropping my head, I envisioned a steadfast hand clasping my own. With fresh resolve, I followed the group to our jungle abode.

After a light supper and unpacking, I dutifully practiced my shot-giving techniques using an orange, needle, and syringe. "Here are a few Yuquí phrases that will be helpful to you," Alan said, handing me several printed cards. He drilled me on pronouncing the words correctly using the right intonation. *"Basa juä nderasi?"* (Where does it hurt)? *"Taretocho."* (Let me give you a shot). *"Emoquiö."* (Swallow this pill).

The day had been exhausting. I gazed out the screened window to admire a cascade of shade spilling over the deepening emerald-green jungle. The setting sun painted the Chimoré River in deep, rich tones of brown. It was time to call it a day. Following a shower with the trusty bucket and cup in a plastic-lined stall, we dragged ourselves to bed. Alan showed me how to secure the mosquito netting beneath the mattress before we surrendered to fatigue and drifted into deep sleep.

★★★★★★★

Stabbed!

*You stabbed me, then pretended
you were the one bleeding!*

The following morning, I woke to the sounds of a rainforest symphony. The hum of cicadas joined successions of trills, chirps, buzzes, and whistles, all announcing the presence of countless jungle creatures greeting the new dawn. I yawned and rubbed my eyes, taking a moment to remember where I was. My awareness began to dawn with the morning; this was my inaugural day serving God in the great Amazon jungle. I lingered in bed, enjoying the rainforest's concerto for a few more moments before jumping out to get dressed.

Arriving to our side of the river

While sipping on my makeshift brew of instant coffee, I looked out the screened kitchen window to see the Chimoré River flowing at a near distance. Dick Strickler had just arrived at the riverbank with a motorboat full of our dark-skinned friends. Alan dashed out the door and sprinted down the beach to assist them. In those initial years, the Yuquí spent their nights camped across the river from the base and were transported to our side on a daily basis.

Sometime later, the group wanted to move and settle on the missionary's side of the river.

I gulped my coffee down and tried to reign in a bundle of nerves, then dashed out the door to head over to the clinic. As I approached,

I saw a group of Yuquí already gathered around the clinic porch. *Nothing like beginning the day in full swing!* I groaned. Whispers and giggles ensued as I made my way up the steps to unlock the door. Eager eyes watched my every move; after all, this was Alan's new bride!

After reviewing Jane's instructions listing the names and treatments to be administered, I stepped out the door and beckoned my first patient. A frail older lady stood up and laboriously climbed the few steps into the clinic; long strands of graying hair framed

Vickie at the clinic

her brown wrinkled face. This was the esteemed matriarch of the clan. Gesturing her to a seat, I sanitized and prepped for the shot, reminding myself to double-scrub her soiled arm with alcohol-drenched cotton.

Vickie at the clinic

With penicillin drawn and air bubbles banished, I faced my charge and turned to eye my patient. She seemed to be made up of more bones than flesh. Determined to be gentle, I pinched an inch of her arm and inserted the needle delicately, like pricking a baby's tender skin. The nasty thing rebounded as if it had hit a hard, rubber basketball. Grandma didn't bat an eye. *She must be one tough cookie,* I thought. *The needles easily pierced the thick-skinned oranges I practiced on.*

"Remember: inject the needle at a sharper angle with a swift motion of the wrist. The quicker it goes in, the less it hurts." Jane's words echoed in my mind like she was right over my shoulder directing my every move. So, there I was, thumb and forefinger gripping with the needle angled like I was aiming at a bullseye. I flicked my wrist with the speed of a ninja and launched that needle in a scene worthy of a slapstick comedy. Totally missing the mark, I ended up giving myself an impromptu acupuncture session; a piercing pain alerted my unsuspecting digit of the surprise attack! It was everything I could do to squelch a deafening *"OOOOOUCH!"* Abruptly, I turned my back to the patient as blood spurted from my throbbing thumb. Grandma? She sat cool as a cucumber on her perch, oblivious to my comedy of errors. A quick wrap job with gauze and tape, and I was back in business.

"... and act like you know what you're doing! You'll soon be giving shots like a pro," Jane's words taunted me. I turned around feigning expertise. This was all just part of the medical procedure!

Grandma sat patiently on the stool like a lamb to the slaughter, trusting her inexperienced nurse completely. After all, this was Alan's new bride! She was convinced these amazing shots were healing her infection, and she felt better every day.

In a slight panic and acutely aware that I would have to attempt a third try at injecting her arm, I silently cried out in desperation to the Lord, *"Please Father, I need your help!"* No sooner had I breathed my prayer than an article I had read about a more proficient technique of giving shots came immediately to mind: Stretch the skin taut rather than pinching it together. I decided to give it a try. I stretched the skin on Grandma's arm tightly, aimed carefully, and swiftly injected the needle. The needle glided in effortlessly, like it was piercing a ripe peach. As the saying

Beloved Grandma of the clan

goes, "Third time's a charm!" The injection was so seamless, Grandma hardly noticed I had pulled it off.

Once a band aid was applied, the aged woman slowly arose from the stool. She shuffled towards the door, but not before turning and shooting me a broad, affectionate smile. That nagging infection of hers was nearly gone and it was all due to these *amazing* shots! From that day forward, I administered injections like a pro!

Yiti Afuera!

Curiosity aroused; I couldn't help but wonder: What on earth was all the commotion about? Stepping outside, I saw a Yuquí girl dashing towards the house screaming at the top of her lungs *"Yiti afuera! Yiti afuera!"* Recognizing *Yiti* as a Yuquí word referring to a small child or baby and *afuera* as Spanish for outside, I was momentarily perplexed to see no children outdoors. Then it hit me like a bolt of lightning. Grabbing the little black box from inside the house, I hightailed it for the bamboo shed casting anxious eyes heavenward. *LORD, PLEASE! I really need Your help!*

Bamboo shed

Upon entering the shed, I discovered the woman had already delivered and saw that the yiti was most definitely *afuera* (outside). The newborn lay eerily still, coated in a bluish-white film. *Could it be stillborn?* Anxiously, I drew in for a closer look. The rhythmic rise and fall of the baby's chest reassured me she was breathing. Following Jane's well written instructions, I inspected the placenta to make sure it was whole and intact, then, felt the umbilical cord, which still throbbed with life-giving blood. This was my cue to get some clean water, soap, fresh garments, and linens from the house. Returning, I found the cord's pulse had stilled.

Once I tied the baby's umbilical cord and cut it with sanitized scissors; I cleansed the infant's tummy and secured her belly button with a medicated bandage. She was then gently washed, diapered, and swaddled in a soft flannel blanket. After cleaning up the mother and ensuring she was comfortably settled in a freshly made bed, I placed the newborn next to her mother's breast.

Gratefully, I gazed at the resting mother and child, feeling jubilant. *Quite impressive for a mere fortnight's experience!* I mused. The whole process had gone seamlessly and my heart was full of praise and thanksgiving to God for His divine assistance. Postpartum shots were then administered to prevent infection. I returned home to prepare a meal for the mother, then left that evening with everything in good order. The woman's teenaged slave girl was left in charge for the night and would alert me if anything seemed amiss.

The following morning, I entered the bamboo hut, carrying a warm bowl of sweetened oatmeal and fruit for the mother. She enjoyed her breakfast while her little one rested peacefully by her side. After eating, she lay back down to rest, but not before gesturing towards a nearly brimming bedpan. *Oh dear!* I groaned inwardly, *Jane didn't mention this part in her notes.* Unbeknownst to me, the woman's slave girl standing just outside the door was expected to do the dirty work; but being the inexperienced jungle bride that I was, I retrieved the bedpan like a dutiful nurse. Chalk it up for humble servanthood!

Clutching the bedpan as far from my nose as humanly possible, I inched forward, one painful step after another. The bemused mother watched with apparent apprehension as I stretched my arms to the limit towards the screen door and carefully crept forward. I still had the daunting task of trekking it 100 feet down to the outhouse once I made it outside the shed. Just as I was steadying myself to open the door, a worn-out spot in the old palmwood floor gave way under my foot.

"AAARRRGGHH! Why Lord? Why me?" I cried echoing the Yuquí mother's vociferous exclamation of *"Eturaaambiti!"* (That's not good! That's not good at all!) The baby joined our distraught chorus with bawls and loud cries.

Thoroughly disgusted, I pulled my damp foot out of the hole, shaking my head at the total absurdity of it all, and resisted the temptation to dump the entire contents into its depths. Of course, that would have undermined everything we'd been teaching them about sanitation. With steely resolve and arms rigidly outstretched, I grasped the bedpan, kicked the screen door wide open, and strode out like a sanitation superhero. Leaving the bewildered mother and wailing child behind, I proceeded down the jungle pathway with *intense* concentration. The mother's slave girl stood outside and watched incredulously, looking as perplexed as the mother. Why, this was Alan's wife doing the dirty work for her! She just might like this new bride of his!

Advancing with focused solemnity, I inched forward much like a priestess bearing an offering for her gods. The stretch seemed painfully long, but I faithfully plodded onward until I reached my destination: the outhouse. Dropping off the unsavory load, I zipped quickly to the house.

"You won't believe what just happened!" I hollered to Alan as I entered the back porch where the plastic shower stall was located. "I need you to bring me several buckets of water."

In the shower cubicle, I narrated my adventure to my hubby while engaging in an intense soap opera: scrub, rinse, repeat, scrub, rinse, repeat (you get the drift). After ensuring I was squeaky clean, I emerged from the stall feeling like a brand-new person. Nothing like a good shower to kick off the morning! Donning fresh attire, I was out the door again to tackle more clinic duties.

The following day, as I made my way down the path to the worn-out shed, I tried imagining what life was like for Yuquí mothers giving birth before missionary intervention. The nomadic lifestyle of the

Yuquí led to a high rate of infant deaths, and it was no wonder. During labor, the expectant woman concealed herself behind palm leaves throughout the whole birthing process. It was taboo for any men to be present. Two or three other women accompanied her until the baby began to emerge, then split the scene, leaving the helpless mother alone to fend for herself. Complications were common, such as the umbilical cord strangling the infant or obstructed labor. Cesarean necessities often arose, and it wasn't rare to discover both mother and child had perished. In such cases, a servant girl might be sacrificed to join her mistress in the afterlife. If the deceased was of high

Coming down the trail

status, more than one Yuquí slave might be killed for her spirit's journey. Such were the miserable deceptions and traditions the Yuquí were enslaved to.

I arrived at the bamboo shed and was pleased to find the infant suckling at the mother's breast. Yet, the woman's detached demeanor troubled me; she cradled her child with a disheartening lack of warmth, as if devoid of any love for her new baby daughter. Sons were prized for their future roles as hunters and providers. I wondered if her indifference stemmed from disappointment.

I diligently cared for the newborn and tried to lift the morale of the mother over the following days. The baby seemed well enough, and the mother was extremely anxious to reunite with her spouse and kin across the river. Hoping it would lift her spirits, she was ferried across to her people, accompanied by the infant and her servant girl.

About a week had passed when the father and mother, along with a group of very distressed relatives, arrived on our back doorstep holding a limp and gravely ill baby. Dick Strickler had ferried them over by boat from the other side of the river. Immediately, we sensed the gravity of the situation. The child's faint breath was strained and occasionally stopped altogether. *How can this be?* I questioned, looking on in total shock. *How did the baby's health deteriorate so rapidly?*

The entire group of family entered our house and crammed together in the back room. Anxiously, they watched Alan and me take turns giving the infant gentle mouth to mouth resuscitation. We breathed softly into her delicate, tiny mouth, observing her chest inflate and deflate with each vital breath. In silence, we begged the Lord to save the baby's life. We continued administering the life-giving procedure until, after a long period of persistent effort, we realized the baby was dead. Why had they waited so long before asking for help? And how had the infant's health deteriorated so rapidly? I was certain we could have saved the baby if only they had come sooner.

With tears rolling down his cheeks, Alan turned to tell the anxious group of onlookers that the newborn had breathed her last. My husband embraced the father and mother, grieving with them. Grief-stricken wails peppered with eerie chants to the spirits began to engulf our temporary jungle home. I stood speechless, intensely sobered with the urgency of reaching our Yuquí friends with the Truth of the Gospel. The wicked deceptions of the devil had imprisoned their minds for long enough! Only the light of God's Word could break through their dark misperceptions and unveil the lies to which they were shackled. Only Jesus could break through the profound spiritual obscurity that shrouded them.

> *... the god of this world has blinded the minds*
> *of unbelievers, to keep them from seeing the*
> *light of the gospel... 2 Corinthians 4:4 ESV*

Forward Ho!

A different band of Yuquí warriors had begun making their presence known near another missionary base about sixty miles northeast of our area. The still-hostile nomads' prolonged absence from this jungle base had previously raised concerns, but now that items from the gift racks were disappearing, there was no doubt the nomads were once again roaming the area. And so, our ministry at the Chimoré base faced an unexpected challenge just several weeks after we arrived.

No one on the missionary team at the Hediondo jungle base spoke Yuquí and they urgently needed Alan's help. Thus, just as my budding Spanish studies had terminated so abruptly in Cochabamba, so did my blooming nursing skills at the Chimoré base. The dust had hardly settled when the summons to action echoed once again, driving Alan and his jungle bride onward with the enduring rallying cry of "Forward Ho!"

The Hediondo camp

The flight to our new assignment was not long. As the plane touched down on the green, grassy strip, I noticed the camp was small and the Hediondo River flowing nearby was much less imposing than the grand Chimoré River we had left behind. Nevertheless, the base was well-maintained with four orderly jungle houses beside the riverbank.

Freed from my medical duties at the Chimoré base, I found more time to adapt to jungle life. Alan was familiar with the Hediondo camp, having been part of a team working there during his bachelor days. Despite certain hardships of living in the wild, our love thrived, and we were happy to be together in this adventure.

The Pouncy family

Our neighbors, Wallace and Barbara Pouncy, were former coworkers with Alan and became close friends of ours. We were entertained on a daily basis by the Pouncy's semi-tamed capuchin monkey (the "organ grinder" kind of monkey seen in the movies). DeeDee Bop, as the little monkey was called, was nicely accommodated in a nearby tree between our adjacent houses. He had a sturdy platform to sit on with all the essentials: food, a solid cup with water, and even a toothbrush. Every morning, we stepped out the door with a cup of water and toothbrush in hand and Deedee Bop followed suit by grabbing his own toothbrush hanging from a string. After dipping it into his water cup, he joined us in our daily routine of cleaning our teeth. The only thing he lacked was toothpaste.

Yuquí girl with capuchin monkey

The five of us enjoyed DeeDee Bop's daily antics but the fun was just beginning once the hens were let out to forage. Seeing the chickens nearby, the little monkey purposely dropped crumbs and food from his platform to lure them underneath. Then, with the precision of a marksman, he'd launch his hefty water cup from above. We'd look out to see a feathery explosion of portly hens squawking and running in a hysterical flurry down the airstrip. DeeDee Bop was right behind hopping on all fours in hot pursuit and yapping away with glee. It was pure monkey business and very entertaining.

One hot, sultry day, Alan asked if I'd like to take a boat ride up the Hediondo River for a little outing. The watercraft was nothing more than an unembellished aluminum motorboat used for fishing and hunting, but it may as well have been a sleek sport boat as far as I was concerned. A cool breeze blowing on my damp face during those sweltering hot days was a blessing from above.

We took off, wind blowing our hair, admiring the jungle's lush drapery on both sides of the small river. Alan had learned some excellent hunting skills during his single years, courtesy of his nomadic Yuquí friends. Not long after we left, he throttled back and whispered, "Can you smell those pigs?"

"Pigs?" I responded in astonishment. How could anyone smell pigs going full speed ahead with the wind whipping against our faces? The ever-familiar scent of decomposing vegetation in the rainforest's damp earth seemed to eclipse any other odors.

With a finger to his lips, Alan gestured for me to be quiet, then landed the boat stealthily and secured it to a stout branch. Clad in high jungle boots with the bottom of his jeans snuggly tucked in and armed with a shotgun, he bounded up the steep, muddy bank leaving me as mosquito bait in the boat. Being his ever-loyal sidekick, I quietly sat in the craft; only the buzzing of mosquitoes broke the muggy silence. Those blood-thirsty pests dive bombed me from every angle and the more they assaulted, the more sourly I speculated: *Just how long was this "spur-of-the-moment hunting venture" going to take anyway? So much for that refreshing boat ride!*

White-lipped peccary

It couldn't have been much over fifteen or twenty minutes (an agonizing amount of time when you're hot, cranky, and slapping ravenous mosquitoes) when three loud gun shots startled me. Shortly after that, Alan's smiling face peered from atop the bank where he announced his success in hunting three white-lipped peccaries. Given our closeness to camp, he escorted me back before retrieving the game. That night, the team feasted on fresh jungle pork.

Living in such isolation made hunting and fishing an absolute prerequisite for the missionaries. Basic supplies such as fuel, rice, and flour, along with the occasional fresh produce, were flown in every three to four weeks. For the most part though, we lived off the land. Adjacent to our houses flowed the Hediondo River, and it wasn't uncommon to see our men hauling an alligator up its murky banks following a hunt. The alligator tail is reminiscent of crab meat and quickly became my preferred jungle delicacy. On one particular evening, Alan returned with an unusually large alligator and left the carcass lying on the ground outside of our house overnight. He planned on removing the tail in the morning.

The following day, I ventured out just in time to witness him dismembering the gator's tail with his trusty machete. A bullet hole was visible just above the eye, marking where the creature had been shot. It had sprawled there all night. With considerable force, Alan delivered a decisive blow to the base of its fleshy appendage. Suddenly, the gator's head jerked up and turned to strike him.

"He's alive!" I screamed. The sudden lurch of the gator's head startled even my husband, but after poking and prodding it cautiously, he reassured me the animal was completely lifeless. "He's dead! It's just his nerves reacting," Alan reassured me and proceeded chopping the tail off without any further ado.

Even though the creature was dead, the gator's nerves were putting up a serious last stand! Its hefty tail thrashed about during

Another gator

the whole detachment process and quivered as Alan skinned and cut the meat into bite sized chunks. Finished with that task, he hauled some gator bits inside for me to batter and fry up for lunch.

I dubiously dipped the pieces into egg and seasoned flour and was unnerved to feel a slight quiver. Shooting a worried glance over to my hubby, I blurted out, "Let's stick this gator meat into the freezer overnight. It's still too fresh." (Our humble fridge had a tiny freezer compartment up top.) "Nah, just fry it up," Alan said nonchalantly. "The hot oil will do the trick." With skepticism, I plopped the battered pieces into the hot oil, eyeing them like a hawk as they crackled away. "Was that the oil bubbling or did that piece just twitch?"

After blotting the pieces with a paper towel, I piled the crispy, golden nuggets onto a platter, but not before inspecting each and every piece once again. Seeing nary a quiver, I set the platter next to the fried sweet plantains and rice on the table and announced, "It's time for lunch."

After giving thanks, we served our plates, and I insisted my husband be the first to partake of the crispy fare. I still was not convinced the quiver had been thoroughly quenched. Watching Alan's mouth and expressions studiously, I tried detecting even the slightest grimace on his face. He chewed the first nugget with gusto and then stabbed another. He seemed to relish the second piece as well, probably amused by his wife's intense scrutiny. As he was about to dig into a third piece, Alan looked up from across the table and exclaimed, "Well, are you just going to just sit there and stare? The gator's fantastic!" His confidence was contagious. I braved my first bite and was wowed by the savory crunch and quickly heaped more onto my plate. After serving myself some fried sweet plantains and rice, I bit into another piece, relishing the delicious crispiness. Turning to Alan, I purred "Ahh, there's nothing more delicious than digging into a *fresh* batch of crispy gator nuggets!"

Pups Beware

The sinking sun had cast a golden glow over the shadowing jungle trees surrounding our base. Evening was always heralded by the penetrating crescendo of cicadas, their shrill song growing louder and louder as darkness fell over our camp. Mosquitoes swarmed our screens, their presence a reminder of the jungle wilderness just beyond our walls. Thankful for the protection indoors, we ignited the kerosene lamp and settled down to do some language study.

Vickie studying by the pressure lantern

After a while, the steady drone of the pressure lamp had a tranquilizing effect. My eyes grew heavy, and I struggled to focus on the pages of Yuquí words and definitions before me. We were about ready to call it a day when sharp barks shattered the calm. Immediately, we shifted into high alert mode.

All the team members of the Hediondo jungle base owned dogs. The canines were allowed to roam freely on the airstrip for one hour daily under supervision but remained tethered otherwise, in case the nomads showed up. Our neighbors, the Pouncy's, owned an outstanding dog they called Jill. She was exceptionally smart, obedient, and loyal. Currently nursing a new litter of puppies, Jill was not one to bark at night, making her urgent cries all the more alarming. Her frantic yelps increased in volume and intensity.

Alan rushed outside to join Barbara Pouncy and investigate, flashlights in hand. Jill fitfully emerged from her kennel yelping and whining only to dash back in again. As Alan and Barbara drew near, the whines and cries of her pups grew louder. They gathered the squealing pups in their arms, and hurried inside to see what was wrong under the bright illumination of our pressure lamp. To everyone's horror, we discovered large, dark-brown army ants pinching the tender flesh of the puppies' bellies, navels, and inner thighs.

Barbara joined us in our frenzied efforts to yank off the pinching ants, flinging each one to the floor and smashing them soundly underfoot. After about twenty minutes of mad plucking, the last nasty army ant was yanked off and crushed. Had those aggressive foragers had their way, the puppies' tender flesh would have been nipped off bit by bit with the ant's large scissor-like pincers and hauled away to their food cache. Army ants are highly effective jungle predators and can kill small prey. Due to Jill's keen alertness, we intervened just in time. Within a short while, she was suckling her litter contentedly in the safety of the Pouncy's screened house and we all breathed a sigh of relief.

The ant attack gave a harried finish to our evening routine, and we were ready to call it a day! Alan turned off the pressure lamp, signaling it was time to go to bed. We tucked the mosquito net under the mattress and rested our weary heads on our pillows, then thanked God for His divine protection over Jill's tender brood. The evening drone of the lantern gave way to the gentle symphony of croaks, chirps, and hums from beyond our window screen. Softly lulled by the soothing melody of the jungle wilderness, we drifted into a deep sleep.

Sufficient unto the day is the evil
thereof. Matthew 6:34b KJV

First Appearance

Wallace Pouncy walked right into our house to drop the news: "There are two Yuquí out by the gift rack." Alan headed straight out to welcome the warriors standing at the edge of our clearing. Other men in camp followed suit as they heard the nomads had made an appearance.

Yuquí warrior

Approaching the two Yuquí near the rack, my husband observed a few more warriors down the jungle path; a couple of them had painted their bodies with a deep purple dye from a jungle fruit. They believed it gave them special protection. The duo at the rack were slaves and were sent on ahead as a safety check. Alan greeted them warmly with Yuquí phrases of friendship and called to the warriors down the path. After conversing with those further away, he tried coaxing them over to the gift rack, but they weren't having it. *"De tu eyu!"* (You come here!) was their immediate response.

Most of the missionary men had turned up with bananas by then. The nomads on the trail looked chill enough and nonaggressive, so the team suggested Alan take a stalk of bananas as a gift and meet the nomads farther down the path. So off he went, bananas in tow, to greet the tribal bigwigs.

As he interacted with the group, Alan concluded that one of the warriors decked out in purple paint was the leader. The Yuquí warrior looked very much like the chief back at the Chimoré base and had a distinct air of authority about him. Later, Alan pieced together that there were two master/slave dynamics going on, as well as two nice-looking young warriors who appeared to be high-class. He suspected the others were probably all slaves.

Our modest banana patch at the Hediondo was producing poorly which prompted our men to conserve as many bananas as possible. They hoped to entice the Yuquí to return for more. Since bananas do not grow wild throughout the rainforest, the warriors wanted all they could find and had no intention of coming back the following day. Unimpressed by the small amount they received, the chief decided to inspect our banana patch for himself with some of his companions.

Soon the sound of chopping machetes echoed across camp as the nomads hacked away at most of our bananas, even cutting down those that were totally green. After their plunder, they headed back toward the gift rack across the airstrip, where the chief ventured down

Yuquí with their palm leaf packs

the trail leading into the dense jungle. At the end of the trail, Alan saw a woman emerge from the dark shadows to join him and assumed she was the chief's wife. She wore nothing but a baby sling made of bark-rope slung over her shoulders.

Meanwhile, other Yuquí men wandered off in search of more bananas, and although it seemed like the interaction was winding down, Wallace Pouncy was near our sugar cane field at the northwest end of the airstrip, engaging with still other nomads. In a

Woman with bark string skirt

gesture of goodwill, Wallace removed his shirt and presented it to the warriors.

Subsequently, the chief and his group turned around and made their way back to the gift rack, prompting our men to approach and engage in conversation with them once again.

"Have your wife come out and she can meet *Eteguayo* (my childless wife) so they can become friends," my husband suggested. The chief wasn't interested. This made it challenging for Alan to keep the conversation going. Then the subject of hunting came to his mind; now that's a topic that *always* captivates the nomads. "We'll go along the river tonight and shoot meat for you. Come back tomorrow and we will give you the meat," Alan said.

"Shoot a *yiquiareguasu* (caiman, a South American crocodilian) for me," the chief replied.

"Would you like some honey?" Alan asked him, knowing this was a great delicacy for the Yuquí. Wallace Pouncy left and returned with a broad banana leaf generously laden with the sweet nectar. They wanted Alan to try it first, making sure it was safe. Then Wallace brought more for leader number two. The two warriors handed the honey, wrapped in banana leaves, to their slaves to take with them for later. Both leaders promised to return the next day bringing their wives with them.

Alan and Vickie inspecting Yuquí arrow

Within the safety of the Pouncy's house, we missionary wives kept a vigilant eye on things on the other side of the airstrip. It was an absolute thrill for me to witness the interaction going on with the nomads from across our grassy green airstrip. I had been in Bolivia little over a month and was already getting my first glimpse of the hostile warriors we had come to befriend.

The day's events left us hopeful and optimistic. We eagerly awaited the nomads' return, but it was not meant to be.

The Roar of Their Foes

The distant guttural rumbling of caterpillar tractors in the rainforest stirred serious concerns among us. Just days after the nomads had left our camp taking our bananas with them, a crew of Bolivian loggers made a grand entrance right into our base. Their astonishment at seeing us was matched by our own expressions of shock. What they thought would be a deserted logging site had been completely transformed with the arrival of missionaries. The lumbermen stood astonished at seeing four orderly missionary houses lined along the riverbank and a pristine airstrip now gracing their once-forgotten camp.

As the team interacted with the loggers, we learned that starting 50 kilometers south of the Hediondo camp, the jungle had been parceled out for logging operations in search of prized mahogany. At the same time, the Yuquí nomads were trying to exist in this region, but evading the advancing loggers was getting more and more difficult. Uncertain of where the lumbermen might strike next, the warriors stayed vigilant and were always prepared to escape at a moment's notice. It became evident that they needed to flee the area or face their demise at the hands of these intruders.

During the remainder of that dry season, logging activities were rampant. As the machinery's roar dwindled each evening, so did our hopes of reconnecting with the Yuquí. Several months later, the rainy season began forcing the loggers to leave until the next dry spell. Our guys took advantage of the lumbermen's absence and left numerous gifts along the deserted roads extending up to forty kilometers south, in hopes the Yuquí might reappear. Despite their constant vigilance, no evidence was found that the nomads had returned. When the dry season resumed, logging would intensify once again. What should we do?

The team took advantage of the empty logging roads to search for areas where the Yuquí might be roaming. Since the forest dwellers were highly nomadic, this proved to be very challenging. The guys made numerous trips into areas of jungle to investigate firsthand information they had gathered as to where the Yuquí might have fled. On the basis of that information, the men would need to work out plans for future contact endeavors.

Extensive survey trips needed to be made to look for indications as to where the Yuquí might have gone. Frequently, the team had to hack through thick thorny undergrowth with machetes just to make progress. Their packs were heavily loaded with essentials: hammocks, mosquito nets, cooking gear, basic foodstuffs like rice and bouillon, as well as radio equipment to keep in contact with those of us at the Hediondo base. Roughing it in virgin jungle was definitely not for the faint of heart.

As the sole team member conversant in the Yuquí language, Alan's involvement during those survey trips was always crucial. The other husbands alternated doing the surveys with one staying behind to manage the camp and support the wives and children. Alan didn't get that luxury. It was the hottest time of year with temperatures soaring along with the humidity. I was expecting our first child, and the repeated separations were hard on us both.

After numerous separations, we finally got a hiatus when we traveled to Cochabamba for the expected arrival of our firstborn. Three weeks later, my labor started, and I was rushed to the hospital. The delivery proved to be difficult and long (thirty hours of contractions) but eventually the doctor, with forceps in hand, delivered a healthy baby boy. The anesthesiologist praised my doctor's skill, saying that any other obstetrician would have delivered the baby by Cesarean. The only thing amiss was a large swollen blister-like lump at the top of our son's head attesting to the lengthy time he had been in the birth canal. Even with the

swelling, we thought he was the most beautiful baby in the world. The fluid in the bump was quickly absorbed resulting in a perfectly shaped head. We were more than overjoyed with our new son and after several weeks, returned to our jungle home at the Hediondo base.

Alan, Vickie, and baby Sammy

After settling in once again, more survey trips ensued. The separations never became easier, making time together as family all the more precious. Everyone at the Hediondo base kept an eye on the gift rack in hopes that the loggers had not completely scared the nomads out of the region. How well we remembered the thrill of seeing their brown bodies gathered under that gift rack.

Throughout all the surveys made by our men, however, no evidence was found to indicate the Yuquí had returned to our locale. As the months dragged on, our hopes of the nomads returning grew faint. Come dry season, the logging would pick up in earnest once again. Desperately needing God's help in finding the illusive nomads, we untiringly sought the Lord for His wisdom, guidance, and provision with the undertaking.

The Lord answered our prayers in a marvelous way. A missionary helicopter arrived in Bolivia precisely when we most needed their help. When the pilot learned of the contact team's efforts to make friends with the Yuquí, he offered to fly for us for just the cost of the fuel; that cost was equivalent to what we normally paid per hour to fly in the small mission Cessna. What a bargain and what a machine the Bölkow Bo105 turned out to be! It arrived just as the team was making plans to explore remote jungle terrain with no easy access. Thanks to the helicopter, our men were able to explore in a few days an area that would have taken many weeks or even months on foot.

Strategies were made and the team divided into two crews of three men; each had a Christian Yuquí from the Chimoré base, a Yuquí speaking missionary (Bob Garland or Alan Foster) to interact with the Yuquí guide, and a third missionary to complete each squad. They wanted to look over an area along the Chore River which was notorious for the number of hunters and loggers who had been shot over the years by the unfriendly nomads. Clearly, it was an area the Yuquí warriors frequented often.

Beach landing

After arriving at the Chore River by helicopter, a high beach was spotted where the chopper could land and spend the night. The next morning, the aircraft lifted off with one of the teams in search of a small jungle clearing where the helicopter could hover and drop them off. Then the pilot would return to pick up the other crew and do the same. After each day's survey had been completed, the crews hiked back to the riverbank and waited for the rotorcraft to return them to the beach camp for the night. In a few days of hiking across the high belts of jungle, the men "struck gold!"—trails the nomads regularly used during their migratory travels and had traveled recently.

Once those trails were found, it became clear we needed to abandon the work at the Hediondo base and establish a new contact base close to the nomad's customary migratory routes. Plans were put into action to move a team of our men into that region to immediately begin a contact effort. All the years of effort expended at the Hediondo contact base were coming to a close.

Meanwhile, Sammy and I were staying at the mission guest house in Cochabamba, enjoying its comforts yet really struggling with the distance from Alan. The separations were tough, but the sacrifices were necessary in order to reach the Yuquí. Later, we boarded with a Bolivian family so I could immerse myself in Spanish and accelerate my learning of the country's primary language.

Vickie and baby Sammy

After each survey was finished, Alan hightailed it to Cochabamba where he could join me and our baby boy at the mission home. Those reunions were always moments of profound joy for us. My heart always skipped a beat when my husband walked through the large mission gate after being away so long. Still clad in his jungle attire and sporting a bushy black beard (one doesn't bother shaving in the thick of jungle surveys), he looked more like Che Guevara, the Cuban revolutionary, than the clean-shaven veteran I had married. But oh, how my heart skipped a beat when I saw him walk through that gate.

★★★★★★★

The Grand Hotel

Imagine an area of dense jungle roughly the size of Connecticut that's dotted with countless swamps, streams, and rivers. This reflects the expanse of jungle our missionary husbands were trekking through to trace the Yuquís' nomadic paths. Thinking the Military Geographic Institute in La Paz might have aerial photos of this part of the rainforest, Alan arranged a quick trip back to Cochabamba to spend a few days with me and baby Sammy. He planned to zip over to La Paz for a night, hopefully to procure the jungle aerials from the Institute.

Our time together would be short, so I suggested the baby and I accompany him on his brief hop to La Paz (a mere forty-five minute flight). I wanted every moment I could to be with him.

"I would love to have you join me," he declared, "but let me warn you; this is no luxury trip! I've already made reservations in a common peoples' hotel." Finances were tight, ministry expenses steep, and my husband was frugal. Our faith-based mission operated similarly to Hudson Taylor's renowned China Inland Mission.

"We'll be together," I responded, "and that's all that matters! I'd love to see La Paz and it's only an overnight trip. Didn't you say the name of the place you made reservations with was the Grand Hotel? With a name like that, it couldn't be all that bad!" So, it was settled. I packed an overnight bag and the following day we hopped on a flight to La Paz, a.k.a. 'the city that touches the sky'.

Nestled in a canyon and hugged by tall mountains and the sharp, snowy Andean peaks, La Paz could be pictured as sitting at the bottom of a deep bowl. With an elevation close to 12,000 feet above sea level, La Paz is the highest administrative capital in the world.

Mount Illimani overlooking La Paz

The majestic triple-peaked Mt. Illimani, which towers above the city, is always covered in snow.

Touching down at El Alto Airport, we snagged a cab to our lodgings, then zigzagged through snug lanes until we finally halted in front of our destination. "THE GRAND HOTEL" sign shone in bright neon glory above the building.

"See? It doesn't look so shabby," I remarked as the grand sign sparked flickers of hope. We opened the entrance door to step into a huge lobby. The only thing that saved the oversized room from sheer emptiness was a single desk with one lone attendant far at the other side. We checked in and were handed a key with directions to our sleeping quarters; then commenced walking down a very long, very cold, and very narrow corridor. The farther we continued, the gloomier my optimism became.

"Well," chirped Alan, mustering all the cheer he could summon, "this has the right number." He unlocked and opened the door after which we squinted into a small room, and by small, I mean cramped! The room was just big enough to fit two narrow iron cots. One lone bulb dangled from the ceiling, its dirty string begging for mercy. There was nothing else in that stark room, nothing! No lamp, no bedside table, no pictures, no rug, not even color for that matter! Just gray, cold walls and two iron cots with lumpy pillows and blankets that could double as Brillo pads. To have light in the small public bathroom down the hall, we had to remove the lone lightbulb from its fixture and take it with us.

Alan turned to me, his face a picture of apology, and remarked rather sheepishly, "I tried to warn you!" Not admitting that even he could imagine *this* level of economy. I bundled our son in my coat and nestled him beside me on one of the iron cots, ensuring that one of us would stay warm as we braced for the night's adventure in austerity.

Eager to escape our frozen cell early the following morning, we left to grab some hot, delicious café con leche (hot milk mixed with a dab of strong sweet coffee) and freshly baked cheese-covered rolls for breakfast. Yum! With a full stomach, blue sunny skies, and majestic snow-draped mountains surrounding the city, my perspective grew much brighter as we headed over to the Military Geographic Institute.

Once the Institute realized our purpose for obtaining the photos, they were happy to help. They also sold Alan charts of the area so he could carry them along when the team surveyed the jungle. Knowing how valuable the information was, Alan studied them so diligently that eventually he had the maps perfectly memorized right inside his head. Over the coming years, it proved to be worth every minute he spent imprinting those images in his mind.

With maps secured, we set out into the crisp air to explore the heart of La Paz for some sights and local cuisine. The gorgeous Andean peaks were magnificently displayed in the morning sun. Grateful for our late afternoon flight, we savored the scenery and local food.

Our lungs worked hard taking in oxygen as we climbed up and down iconic cobblestone streets and soaked up the Andean culture. We took in an ancient Catholic church's architecture, visited museums, and relished a midday meal at a local eatery. Then it was back to Cochabamba for a few more treasured days with Alan before he set off with his photos and maps for another survey.

Eventually, baby Sammy and I found ourselves flying back to Camp Hediondo. The time had come to bid farewell to our cherished camp and we were once again packing our bags and household items, accompanied with the familiar rallying cry of "Forward Ho!" The camaraderie among the missionaries at this base was precious, and parting ways with our shared jungle home was tough for the entire crew.

A New Jungle Base

The next hurdle our men had to face was figuring out the easiest way to move our base seventy-five miles south to a location on the Víbora River near the migratory routes of the nomads. The team was determined not to depend exclusively on the uncertain availability of the helicopter. They estimated it would be a several-week journey to reach the site by river, which would greatly increase the distance and introduce significant challenges. Nevertheless, it was definitely doable. Once the jungle area was cleared, they could begin building rudimentary houses and have vital supplies brought in by river. Achieving this by helicopter was the much-preferred method, but due to the chopper's indefinite availability, our men needed other means of

Clearing jungle

moving in. They anticipated the undertaking of clearing raw jungle would be very arduous and time-consuming, so sought the help of additional missionary men in the beginning stages.

Meanwhile, pregnant with our second child, I resided at the mission guest home in Cochabamba with our little toddler Sammy. It comforted me knowing my husband could rest assured of our well-being in his absence. Having Alan's sister, Anna, working nearby in the mission finance office was a great solace to me during these separations.

How long the helicopter would remain in Bolivia was uncertain. The pilot had packed up and left the country. When the chopper assisted with searching the higher parts of the jungle, the team had identified a very small jungle village, Puerto Grether, as the nearest point from which to access the new base by land. An old logging track from this village, navigable by swamp tractor, led to the Víbora River allowing us to travel by boat to our new base. In the other direction, the logging track from Puerto Grether connected to the paved road to Santa Cruz.

The new contact base was ten kilometers north of Puerto Grether by helicopter. Situated next to the Víbora River, it was only 4 kilometers from the high belt of land the nomads regularly traveled. When the river was full during the rainy season, we could reach our new camp by boat. During the dry season, when the waterway was too low for boat travel, the camp could be accessed by swamp tractor using the abandoned logging track through the jungle.

Straightaway, our guys began to tackle the formidable job of clearing virgin jungle from the site. Now that the pilot of Helimission had left Bolivia, the helicopter was unavailable for use until another pilot could be found. This left our men totally isolated in the middle of raw jungle without their families and

Alan by a large felled jungle tree

no easy way of getting supplies in. The task of clearing the rainforest turned out to be a much more daunting challenge than anticipated.

From the very start, it seemed the devil had unleashed all his forces to block our men from clearing the land. This was Satan's domain, and he had the Yuquí hopelessly bound in his clutches. God's greatest adversary would make it as formidable as possible to reach this isolated and endangered people group with the hope of the Gospel. Our guys were assaulted by swarms of honeybees and

Bees covering Paul Short's back

hornets and every other stinging insect you can imagine on a daily basis. The jungle was extremely hot and muggy, and malaria finally struck one of our colleagues, Phil Burns, thus, making an urgent evacuation by swamp tractor necessary. The swamp buggy broke down numerous times and the short-term volunteer helpers eventually abandoned the job, finding it way too daunting. One of them was an ex-Green Beret.

None of this stopped our courageous team of men from persevering. Alan was attacked by a swarm of hornets which left his face looking like *Rocky* after a severe boxing match. Even with all the swelling, he pressed on cutting a gift trail with his co-worker, Paul Short. When the two took a momentary break, they heard an eerie noise. Looking to his right, Alan saw a short, creamy, green-mottled viper looking him right in the eye from its perch in a small bush.

The serpent was the shrewdest of all the wild
animals the Lord God had made. Genesis 3:1 NLT

The viper's tail was wrapped around a sapling, and the strange noise they heard was the snake repeatedly trying to strike them. Alan and Paul were just out of reach, but had the viper struck either of them, it would have been in the head or neck and most likely fatal.

For our struggle is not against flesh and blood, but
against the rulers, against the authorities, against the
powers of this dark world and against the spiritual forces
of evil in the heavenly realms. Ephesians 6:12 NIV

The final straw came when our coworker, Wallace Pouncy, lost his balance while felling a large leaning tree on the riverbank and severely cut his wrist on the spinning chainsaw blade. By then, the team was reduced to just Alan, Wallace, and a teammate. In order to transport Wallace to the city, the other two had to make the long and grueling trip by swamp tractor, boat, and then by truck to the city. They had no other choice and deeply regretted having to leave the camp unfinished and with no caretaker.

Returning to Cochabamba, the core team members discussed all the difficulties and adversities they had faced. Remarkably, instead of wanting to throw in the towel, the suffering and troubles only convinced our men all the more that they were encountering fierce opposition from that *serpent of old*. God had already determined to bring the Yuquí to Himself, but evil spiritual forces were equally determined to thwart their endeavors.

After much discussion and heartfelt prayer, the Lord fortified our men to press forward once again and head back out to the jungle. Before they left, Alan and I embraced and murmured our good-byes, weighed down with sadness.

The journey to and from the new site was fraught with challenges; the rainy season had passed, giving way to the dry season which made the river too treacherous to navigate. Clearing the waterway of logs with chainsaws was not only physically draining but also perilous and time intensive. The men's hopes were pinned on the arrival of a new pilot who could man the helicopter and ease the logistical burdens for the crew.

The missionary team was eager to establish a camp that would allow their families to join them, thus ending the prolonged and painful separations; however, for the wives and children, the journey to the new base would be a very long and grueling one. If only Helimission could find a new pilot! This would greatly simplify transporting the families and supplies into the heart of the jungle. We fervently prayed for a new pilot to arrive.

In the meantime, as the men felled large trees and cleared the jungle, the nomads were already making their presence known. When team members checked the gift trails they had previously cut, they discovered footprints in the sand just two hundred yards from their camp. The Yuquí had walked right down the gift trail making no effort to hide their presence. We took this as an indication the nomads knew who our men were and weren't worried about being harmed.

After clearing the jungle, the guys began building rustic jungle houses. Once construction progressed, they explored the surrounding area, wanting to find the best places to hang additional gifts for the nomads. During these explorations, they stumbled upon a mysterious mound of decaying palm leaves, resembling a collapsed palm-thatched structure. This was particularly puzzling as the Yuquí don't construct permanent shelters. Alan felt there had to be a special significance to the structure.

Trailing old Yuquí paths, they encountered several deserted camps, varying in age. It was encouraging to know that the Yuquí had spent a portion of the rainy season camped within just four kilometers of our new contact site. Upon returning to the base, the guys again passed the mound of decaying palm leaves. Light began to dawn on my husband, and he wondered if it could have been a shelter for their dead. His notion was correct.

After the houses were finished, the team carved out enough space in the wilderness for planting bananas or additional houses as needed. With the area cleared and jungle houses erected, the guys were eager to bring in their families; however, they were concerned about the wives and small children enduring the daunting trip overland. They didn't have long to worry about it because our ever-faithful God answered our prayers once again with timely precision. A fresh pilot had just arrived in Bolivia and was ready to command the Bölkow Bo105 helicopter and help move the families. Only God! How we rejoiced and thanked the Lord for His timely provision once again.

The Helicopter

The helicopter approaches closer than any other
(vehicle) to the fulfillment of mankind's ancient
dream of the flying horse and the magic carpet.
Igor Sikorsky

The rhythmic pounding of the helicopter's blades sliced the air with a thunderous intensity: "WHUMPA, WHUMPA, WHUMPA" reverberating through the stifling atmosphere with sensational force. I was relieved the pilot didn't need to execute any of the inverted loops the Bölkow Bo105 was capable of; nevertheless, the ride was nothing short of exhilarating! Two-year-old Sammy's eyes were wide with excitement while his six-week-old sister Becky slept peacefully secured at my breast. As we traveled toward the new Víbora camp, the anticipation of being reunited with my husband added to the day's magic.

Inside the cockpit, the excitement was palpable; young Sammy's eyes sparkled with the thrill of the moment, a shared wonder with his mother. The plexiglass dome offered a panoramic view of the jungle's grandeur below—a wild tapestry of green that stretched as far as the eye could see. My precious children and I were on no ordinary journey; this was a daring escapade deep into the heart of the Amazon jungle. The arrival of a helicopter pilot in Bolivia, precisely when the wives and children needed to be transported to our new jungle base, was nothing short of a miracle, sparing us the demanding and arduous journey through the jungle. With God's timely provision of this remarkable aircraft, our faith took wings.

As I scanned the vast rainforest below, the chances of locating small, isolated groups of Yuquí nomads seemed impossible. One author, after living in the Amazon Rainforest, referred to it as a "Green Hell." From my perspective, it resembled what I imagined the Garden of Eden to look like. I was soon *to* discover how harsh and unkind life can be in that raw wilderness. I tried to imagine elusive clusters of naked nomads roaming the unfathomable expanses below. Finding these small groups of nomads wandering in the rainforest depths was like finding a needle in a haystack.

As for the Yuquí, just struggling to find food in the wilderness was daunting enough; but now, outsiders invading their territory wanted to kill them. Their longstanding plight of trying to survive in the jungle looked more and more grim.

From a human perspective, the *Bia*'s prospects seemed utterly hopeless, yet God was observing these beleaguered tribes with an unfathomable depth of love and mercy that's far beyond our earthly understanding. Surrounded by locals who labeled them as nothing but uncultured "savages," many nationals dismissed them as worthless. There were even calls to deploy the military to eliminate these naked "savages" once and for all. But God above was saying:

> *Who dares despise the day of small things, since*
> *the seven eyes of the Lord that range throughout*
> *the earth will rejoice... Zechariah 4:10 NIV*

Indeed, their Creator would rejoice! Each Yuquí soul is precious and valuable to God; so much so, He shed His blood to save them. Some of those wandering Yuquí individuals later embraced faith in Jesus as their Savior and became His very own children. His gift of salvation is free not only to the Yuquí, but to anyone who will believe and embrace His teachings.

Contemplating the panorama below, I realized anew that a cosmic war was taking place in the jungle's depths. We weren't the only ones hard after the souls of the Yuquí.

Consider how precious a soul must be when both
God and the devil are after it. Charles Spurgeon

We had covered approximately 120 air miles, when the pilot's voice came through the headphones: "We should see the Víbora camp very shortly. We're getting close." Observing the numerous coils twisting and turning in the small waterway below made it clear why the river is called the *Víbora*, which translates to *serpent* or *viper* in English.

The aviator pointed to a tiny, cleared area next to the river that was shielded on three sides by water, protecting the new camp from the Yuquí who did not swim. The fourth side opened to the jungle, with a cleared stretch leading to a gift rack.

A sharp increase in the loud slapping of the blades indicated the helicopter was putting down. After the rotor blades came to a complete stop, I stepped out of the chopper with our two small children. Looking around at the austere surroundings, I suddenly

The helicopter

felt the weight of our new assignment. I had arrived at the frontline of missionary undertaking, where faith meets the conflict.

The camp itself was raw, untouched by the softening hand of greenery; its primal essence a stark contrast to the verdant jungle we had flown over. My subsequent disenchantment with the camp's rough stages of development underscored the beginning of what would be the most challenging years for me.

From afar, my husband hastened to welcome us, and I embraced him warmly, hiding any feelings of disenchantment at the rudimentary surroundings. The men had faced life-threatening challenges to clear the new base and our reunion, after enduring numerous times apart, filled us with much joy and gratitude.

Our jungle home consisted of three rooms, with two designated for sleeping and the third serving as a combined kitchen and living area. The firm earthen floor remained solid until the river breached its bank years later. Furnishings were simple: a table, benches, and storage made from the surrounding wilderness, complemented by a few pieces of plywood for crucial areas. A functional kitchen sink, fed by a rainwater barrel, was a notable addition, although we resorted to river water during the dry spells.

To brighten our dwelling, I adorned the screened windows with handmade blue curtains. A hammock and some outdoor chairs for relaxation served as living room furniture. It marked the beginning of our life in this secluded wilderness.

Washing clothes in a James washer

A few days later, the helicopter made a return trip, bringing essential supplies to the missionaries: kerosene refrigerators and gasoline-powered laundry machines. We rejoiced that the days of resorting to a hand-powered James clothes washer were over. The arrival of the large cargo by helicopter left an indelible impression on my mind, one I will never forget.

The aircraft could be heard from miles away, the atmosphere throbbing with the steady rhythm of the chopper's mighty blades: "WHUMPA, WHUMPA, WHUMPA." The slapping grew louder and louder when suddenly, out of the blue, the helicopter emerged from around the riverbend in full living color! Azure sky and emerald-green jungle made a vivid backdrop for the magnificent orange and white Bölkow Bo105 helicopter's appearance.

Suspended beneath it, a vast net oscillated imposingly, burdened with hefty freight which also contained our kerosene-powered re-frigerator. The chopper's thunder-ous beating soon became a mighty roar hovering right above our camp, as the pilot skillfully deposited the load. With the mighty reverberation of the rotor, he then lifted and set-tled the chopper onto a cleared he-lipad next to the river.

Arriving with another net load

The helicopter service wasn't the only indication of God's providential care for us out there in the jungle wilderness. We rejoiced to hear of the completion of a logging "road" leading to the small settlement of Puerto Grether, just ten kilometers south of our camp. The road was nothing more than a deep mud track during the rainy season, but with our swamp buggy, we could travel if necessary. Fortunately, the lightweight buggy with its aluminum trailer could swim the water-filled gullies along the way.

This alternative means of transportation was vital to us when the helicopter was not available, and traveling by swamp tractor was preferable to hiking through dangerous jungle or traveling by river. The Víbora River could be swift and log-filled, making it too dangerous for the wives and small children to travel. Both the helicopter's arrival and the completion of the logging track were affirmations of God's care for us as we began a new chapter in the heart of the Amazon rainforest.

The Víbora River was known for its population of electric eels which added an element of wonder and caution to the camp. Nestled in the river's natural fortification on three sides, we often watched electric eels come to the surface of the water to breathe. To the north, the dense jungle stood as a barrier, its canopy filtering the sunlight to the camp's bare ground. Jungle houses stood on the northeastern bank of the river where the ground rose gently, providing a vantage point over the water's edge. The constant hum of the rainforest critters and the occasional crackle or gurgle from

the river served as reminders of the vibrant ecosystem that surrounded us, teeming with life both seen and unseen.

Initially, I cooked over a two-burner Coleman camp stove. When baking bread, a metal camp oven could be unfolded and placed over the burners. Jungle camp training had been beneficial in preparing me for the rigors of pioneer missionary work, but as a single girl, it had been fun. The shift from a six-week adventure in the Wisconsin woods to surviving

Alan with electric eel on the right

long-term in the Amazon's wilderness with a baby and small toddler to care for was anything but fun.

★★★★★★★

Eternal Realities

I slapped my hand at the pesky gnats gnawing at my arm. Small as a pinhead, the minuscule *no-see-ums* weren't noticed until they walloped a bite that itched for hours. Sadly, they were microscopic enough to fly right through our window screens and some mosquito netting.

It was another typically sweltering day at the Víbora contact base. In the shade of our home, indoor temperatures reached almost ninety while the outdoor temperature surpassed 100°F. Perspiration beaded my brow as I prepared a meal on the fiery camp stove. I was eager to feed the family and then let our toddlers, Sammy and Becky, cool down with a playful splash in our large blue laundry tub.

After washing the dirt off of some freshly harvested yucca (a.k.a. manioc or cassava, a tubular root tasting similar to potato), I stripped the woody exterior, chopped up the white fibrous flesh, and dumped the pieces into a pot to boil. Then I battered some fish filets and lowered them into the sizzling oil in the cast iron skillet.

Having a kerosene-powered refrigerator in this "no man's land" was a godsend, allowing me to freeze small packages of wild meat or fish in the small box at the top. Alan was an excellent hunter and frequently supplied us with wild pigs and deer, and occasionally the succulent *jochi pintado* (lapa, a small rodent that tastes like a tender, moist piglet). Sometimes he had the good

Alan with tapir

fortune of shooting a tapir. This beef-like animal was large enough to fill all the missionaries' freezers on the base.

Hmmm... sure hope there's enough banana sauce for dessert. I muttered to myself while scanning through plastic containers in the fridge. By shredding sweet plantains and simmering them with a little water, sugar, cinnamon, and a hint of lemon, the sauce made a cool, applesauce-like treat.

Suddenly Sammy's voice broke the silence, "Mommy, Becky spilled her drink." Turning around, I saw the liquid dribbling from the table down to the earthen floor, which conveniently absorbed it. No worries. I regularly dampened the ground to maintain a hard, solid surface.

While piling up dirty dishes, a large roach, of which there were many, scrambled for refuge between the shelf and counter. "Ugh, not another one!" I wailed and grabbed the designated wooden spoon to whop it, only to cringe at the crunch beneath. "I *hate* roaches!" I whined to myself. The day had been an especially trying one for me.

Glancing out the screened window, I saw Alan coming in from cutting the gift trail. The sweatband around his forehead was drenched and his shirt, soaked in perspiration, clung to his torso. He had devised a routine of draping his sweat-soaked, long-sleeve shirts on the clothesline throughout the day, ensuring a dry one was available for him to slip into before entering the house. Clothed in a dry work shirt, he stepped inside. Despite regular washing in our gas-operated wringer washer, the shirts' pale gray hue had darkened significantly due to the rampant mildew flourishing in the jungle humidity.

I was still feeling the effects of my husband's recent discovery of tiny red mites (chiggers) multiplying in the lush green grass that had finally flourished outside our house. The addition of tender green ferns had transformed the outside of our jungle abode into a cheerful looking oasis. I was really bummed that the verdant display would be killed with herbicide the following morning. It had to be done. Chigger bites trigger an intensely itchy and irritating rash. Even the few chickens we had procured had stopped laying eggs due to the distress caused by these parasites.

Over time, our now bare dirt yard eventually welcomed a quaint jungle gym which Alan had constructed from smooth bamboo poles. Complete with a swing suspended from a tree as well as a sandbox, the stark yard at least provided a place for our children to play during times of fewer mosquitoes. But it did little to beautify the place. I longed for a patch of loveliness to adorn our jungle dwelling. *Why God? Why did you choose someone who craves beauty to serve You in this mold and cockroach-infested place?* I grumbled beneath my breath. My attitude only grew bleaker.

I was grateful for the excellent way my husband had fortified our jungle house, ensuring that most chewing insects, snakes, and other unwelcome guests, including the dreaded vampire bats, remained outdoors. He fitted a sink connected by a garden hose to a large barrel which gathered rainwater from the metal roof, thereby providing the convenience of running water at the kitchen sink. With time, living conditions improved, but how I yearned for a touch of beauty during those initial days at our fledgling camp.

"Supper is ready," I announced, setting the table. Gathered around, we clasped hands and bowed our heads, and thanked God for the day's strength and delicious meal before us. The crispy fish paired with the tender yucca was delicious!

After supper, I placed a bucket of water on the two-burner stove to prepare bath water for the children when my gaze fell on the blue curtains hanging on the kitchen window. Just like Alan's shirts, they were succumbing to a dreary gray, particularly at the edges. Despite my diligent efforts with vinegar and baking soda, the mildew always made an unwelcome return. *So much for trying to make things look pretty!* I grumbled to myself; my disposition was about as gray and bleak as Alan's shirts.

Our two young toddlers enjoyed pouring water from plastic squeeze bottles in the big blue laundry tub I bathed them in. Lathering their hair in fragrant tear-free shampoo and wrapping their squeaky-clean bodies in clean jammies was just as therapeutic for me as it was for them.

Disposable diapers were not an option in the jungle, and not even available in Bolivia at that time. Alan ingeniously devised a drying rack above our refrigerator, using the escaping heat to dry cloth diapers during relentless rainy seasons. With careful planning, I kept a very small supply (only two or three) of clean diapers ready for use. At the end of the day with the children tucked in bed, I would wearily sink into our hammock, our makeshift easy chair, and lose myself in the pages of "Mommy of the Mixing Bowl," a gift from Alan's mother. This biography of Doris Aldrich captured heartfelt stories of life with her nine children on a sprawling farm and offered spiritual insights that resonated *deeply* with me. Many of her writings were published in the Moody Monthly magazine of bygone days.

As I settled in, my eye caught sight of ugly mildew forming on the curtains next to the hammock, black mold creeping into their corners. It *really* irritated me and made me feel totally defeated in trying to prettify our jungle home. *Why God? Why did you choose someone who craves beauty to serve You in this mold and cockroach-infested place?* I grumbled to myself. Aware of how quickly self-pity can turn to bitterness, I silently pleaded *Please Lord, I really need Your help to overcome being swallowed up with negativity. I can't do this without You.* With that, I surrendered my complaints and frustrations and turned the page to begin a new chapter in *Mommie of the Mixing Bowl.*

"Of course, Daddy didn't mean to leave the stair gate unlocked, but in all the morning rush, he did. Net-net, the toddler, took advantage of it and scrambled eagerly up to the bathroom with its delightful, forbidden water faucets.

Minutes flew by in characteristic, school-morning fashion. Jan and Jon raced out to the car, in again for lunch-money and out again, slam-banging the door. Daddy gathered up his briefcase and kissed the buttery, crumb-covered children and dashed out the door. (Upstairs the water ran... and ran.) Mommie untied bibs, washed sticky hands and faces, made and remade mental lists: "Things-I-ought-to-do-today" and "Things-which-must-be-done" all accompanied by sudden rushes to save that glass of milk from spilling. (And the water ran... and ran...)"

"Suddenly down it came thru the cap on the living-room ceiling where the old light fixture used to be. Mommie took one look and raced for the stairs. The hall was flooded, the twin's bedroom was a-wash, and the bathroom... Net-net was abundantly satisfied and wading around like a fat, squat duck. She waved a dripping towel and grinned."

I laughed right out loud imagining the scenario.

"Mommie was in no mood for hilarity. Her day was already too full, and this extra work seemed almost unbearable. A rush of resentment and of stinging tears came. She grabbed pads, sheets, and towels from the morning laundry pile to sop up all the water. The hall rug had to be taken up and it seemed that the old wet faded thing matched the grayness of her spirit."

"Why, oh why, do I have to live in this old run-down house!" she complained. She hated the paint-worn stairs, the worn-out curtains, the old furniture and queried tearfully, "Why do I have to love beautiful things and then have to live in such a place..."

Wow! That last paragraph *really* caught my attention! Hadn't I just expressed the exact same complaints to God about my own dreary surroundings? It definitely wasn't by chance that I found myself engrossed in this specific narrative on such an evening. The Holy Spirit was clearly guiding my focus.

"She yanked at the bedroom chest of drawers and jabbed her broom at the dust behind it. ...And there they were—all unsuspected—nine red 'butter tokens.' Mommie picked them up and gazed curiously at them. 'My, what they would have meant during rationing,' she thought, 'but they are of no value now.' And then it came to her all in a flood (not of water but of thoughts!) '... of no value now....' What difference would the old rag rug make 'over there' where all the glory is? Who would care about the battered table in the shining beauty of 'things prepared for us?' And the paint-worn stairs and the old jumped-on couch with the blanket to cover its threadiness. Would they matter in that lovely place? Would any 'thing' be of value—over there?

With a rush she gathered back to the warmth of her heart the seven babies and what they were going to be. She accepted the old house, the floods of difficulties... and water, and the too-full daily round of work. She gathered them back and thankfully so."

I put the book down. By now, not only was my heart humbled but it was aglow with gratitude; hadn't I just pleaded with God to change my souring attitude? *Thank you, Father, for redirecting my focus to things that really matter.* Being so caught up with the fleeting griefs and annoyances of jungle life, I had failed to see the eternal worth of spreading the glorious news of the Gospel to the unreached Yuquí people.

Years after this incident, an airstrip had been installed at the Víbora base. Dear friends came to visit us at our jungle base to bid us farewell before their return to the U.S. The wife, gleaning inspiration from a home decor magazine, was looking for ideas to fix up their future home in the States. While she was engrossed in the glossy magazine atop our makeshift jungle table, I was preoccupied with cooking lunch on our modest two-burner stove. Out of the blue, she turned to me, her expression one of thoughtful regret. "Vickie, I am sorry for being so insensitive. It must be difficult for you to see me browsing through these Better Homes and Gardens magazines while having to rough it out here in the jungle," she said.

My heartfelt reply was a resounding "Not at all!" The transformation within me during those later years was so profound that the allure of beautiful houses held no sway over me. The lessons God was teaching me during those initial years at the Víbora had taken hold.

By then, I had concluded that only two things hold eternal value on this earth: the human soul and God's Word. Our purpose was to connect the lost Yuquí souls with God's Living Word, driven by a deep conviction to share a message of redemption and hope with those among them who were desperately searching for something beyond their current existence. They just didn't realize it was Jesus.

Homespun Hatchery

He plunked down on the table a battered aluminum kettle which looked like it had seen better days. It was accompanied by an assortment of eggs, clean rags, and a thermometer. I eyed my husband curiously, perceiving he was ready to hatch a new idea.

"Whatcha up to?" I inquired.

"I'm going to hatch some chicks."

"Hatch chicks?" I echoed; my voice mixed with bewilderment.

"Yep."

Alan meticulously arranged the rags and thermometer in the old kettle and nestled the eggs inside like precious treasures. Without another word, he stepped out to the backyard. Soon the rhythmic pounding of a hammer could be heard. Returning with a narrow plank, he promptly affixed it above our kerosene fridge where heat was released. Methodically, he hammered in a series of nails, creating a neat vertical line at the top of the board. The old kettle found its new home dangling from one of these nails, as if it were the latest invention of DIY poultry incubation.

"You're really serious about this, aren't you? Sure seems like a peculiar way of hatching eggs."

"Uh huh."

For a full week, Alan busied himself peering inside that old kettle, meticulously adjusting the eggs six or seven times a day. Curiosity finally got the best of me, so I inquired about his constant rotation of the eggs as well as raising and lowering the kettle. "It's all about keeping the kettle at the right temperature," he explained. "We just might have some chicks in a couple of weeks."

I let out a hearty *Ba joria!* which is Yuquí for "You're full of baloney!" "Just *'yolking'* Sweetie," I quipped, and turned to give him a big grin while I secretly admired his determination. He smiled back with an expression that said, "Just wait and see!"

Not a whit disheartened by my pessimistic jesting, Alan cared for his little "eggies" with more devotion than the best of mother hens. Raising and lowering the old aluminum kettle turned into a daily ballet, first high, then low, now in the middle, the location on the nails always being directed by the temperature on the thermometer. I hoped the eggs wouldn't crack up to be rotten after all his devoted effort.

While the eggs incubated, my husband kept busy juggling outdoor tasks with Yuquí language learning at his makeshift indoor study. Meanwhile, I juggled the three (or is it four?) C's: cooking, cleaning, and childcare. Keeping our little ones entertained within the confines of our jungle home was a challenge for sure, especially when the sweltering heat and mosquitoes barred outdoor play. Yet, the sight of their daddy, the ever-diligent egg-turner, provided a delightful diversion to their day. Their eyes sparkled with intrigue as they watched him tend to his eggs. "In just a few days, we might see some chicks hatch," he said one day as the children gazed into the kettle's depths.

"Now Sweetheart, don't count your chickens before they hatch," I quipped. "You might get their hopes up for nothing." Still an unbeliever, I seriously doubted we'd see live chicks popping out of that old aluminum kettle.

I checked to see if my loaves of bread dough were ready to bake, then ignited the camp stove and placed the tin oven on top. It wasn't long before the scent of fresh bread wafted through our quaint rainforest abode.

Day 21 was *finally* crossed off the calendar, signaling the last day of my husband's egg-warming venture. I considered shouting out a loud "WHOOP DEE DOO!" but refrained. I was very eager to get rid of all the chick-hatching paraphernalia from above the fridge! Nonetheless, I patiently waited for Alan to discover his experiment was not all that it was cracked up to be.

"Hey, come take a look," he called out later that morning as he carefully studied the contents of the kettle. The children and I drew near to look inside.

"Do you see it?"

"See what?"

With the tip of a pencil, Alan gingerly drew our attention to a teensy-weensy tip of gray emerging from a minute hole in one of the shells. It was barely visible, but the tiny tip was moving! I was astonished! Why, there was life inside that egg! As time passed, more minuscule beaks started to break through their enclosures. I could hardly believe my eyes!

Soon, Alan lowered the kettle to reveal the first chick struggling to break out of its shell. The soggy fledgling, far from the storybook's plush yellow illustrations, appeared absolutely exhausted and limp. Anticipating fluffy-yellow chicks like the pictures in their story book, Sammy and Becky's excitement certainly didn't match my own. I was utterly captivated!  The very eggs I would have scrambled for breakfast had, in a mere three weeks, morphed into breathing, peeping, living chicks: all within the confines of our fridge's old aluminum kettle. *That man of mine was a GENIUS!* Within a few hours, the hatchling's dry fluff bulked up to twice their size, much to the children's delight, matching the storybook depiction of fluffy-yellow chicks after all.

With the elation of smashing success surging through his veins, Alan got right to work on his next project. My heart sank as I watched him drag chicken wire, small poles, an old lantern and feed containers for water and meal into the house. That corner that housed our blue plastic-rope lawn chair, a box of toys, two pairs of children's flip flops, and a small basket of mending would be turned into a brooding pen. That beat-up old aluminum kettle hanging on a nail behind the fridge was immediately restocked with more fertilized eggs and the chick-hatching paraphernalia multiplied a hundredfold right before my eyes.

*"What **are** you doing?"* I queried with a stern frown on my face as all hope of cleaning up the chick-hatching gear dissipated right before my eyes.

"The chicks are too small to survive outside. We'll need to keep them in the house for a few weeks until they're strong enough to go to the outside pen."

Before long, the brooding pen was ready, and Sammy and Becky gleefully helped their daddy carry the new yellow fluffs to the pen. The children were so overjoyed with the new brood of peeping chicklets that my mommy heart melted (just a little). *Well, at least the chicks are bringing real joy to the kiddoes,* I consoled myself. Nestled away in their fresh abode, the chicklets gathered under the tender watch of their surrogate mom, a lit kerosene lantern, which provided soothing warmth and hushed their anxious chirps. They cozied close to its warm and comforting glow. "Ahh, just look at how contented they've become." I remarked and my mommy heart melted even more.

Our children devoted countless hours to their feathered friends, cradling the downy chicks in their hands and showering them with kisses. Their joy mirrored that of their father's as they took pride in nurturing the young brood. As the chicks grew, they graduated to the outdoor coop, and much to my chagrin, the cycle was renewed with a fresh set of hatchlings in the brooding pen. Soon enough, our outdoor enclosure was bustling with life and the indoor clutter had *at last* been cleared away.

Becky and Sam enjoying their chicks

Our toddler Sammy showed a deep affection for one homely white chicken that had hatched in the old aluminum kettle, despite its lowly status in the pecking order. Its skinny orange legs hung to Sammy's knees as our little boy carried his beloved pet around camp, kissing it tenderly every chance he got. The chicken, scruffy and missing many feathers, might not have been a prize-winner but it was Sammy's dearly beloved pet no matter how tatty it looked.

Eventually, our flock of chickens grew large enough to share with our jungle colleagues. Both chickens and eggs were plentiful, all thanks to that *INGENIOUS*, egg-warming husband of mine.

★★★★★★★

A Freezer on Wheels Experience

You shall remember that the Lord your
God led you all the way...
Deuteronomy 8:2 NIV

What began as a trivial toothache quickly intensified into a severe abscessed tooth. Even the strongest painkillers available in our medical kit couldn't quell the persistent, throbbing pain that deprived me of sleep for three straight nights. The side of my face swelled to a disturbing degree, a particularly concerning development considering our isolated location in the depths of the jungle.

After Alan consulted with doctors by HF sideband radio, we were advised to seek medical help without delay. The severity of the abscess risked spreading infection to my brain, a danger heightened by my four-month pregnancy with our third child. In the absence of an airstrip, Alan attempted all day to secure a helicopter for my evacuation, but without success. Confronted with a grueling fifteen-hour trip to Santa Cruz, and my worsening condition, we could only entrust our predicament into God's hand and pray.

Using the swamp tractor, the journey for medical help required a twelve-hour ride through deep, muddy ruts and swamps, followed by a three-hour drive to the city by road. We had no other choice but to make the drive. Resolutely, Alan prepared to take me to Santa Cruz, a fifteen-hour trip even in optimal conditions.

One of the logging roads

The thought of undertaking such an arduous journey after several sleepless nights troubled me as the pain intensified.

In need of relief, I asked Alan to have our colleagues lay hands on me that evening and pray for God to relieve my pain. A young man assisting at the Víbora initially considered a toothache too trivial to warrant laying on hands and praying. However, upon seeing the swollen condition of my face, he quickly grasped the gravity of the situation. That evening, the men anointed me with oil and prayed fervently, reciting James 5:14–15. Miraculously, the throbbing pain subsided shortly after their prayer session, giving me a much-needed restful night of sleep. Alan and I slept so soundly that we missed our alarms the next morning. Our coworker Larry Depue, who would travel with us, woke us up and we set off about 4:30 a.m. into the dawn.

As we ventured into the heart of the rainforest, the pungent odor of decomposing vegetation gave evidence of the frequent rains we had been receiving; some areas on the track were completely flooded. Thanks to the swamp tractor's gigantic tires, we made it through numerous flooded areas. I whispered a heartfelt, *Thank you,* to my Heavenly Father for having calmed the stabbing pain in my jaw.

The swamp tractor

We hadn't traveled long when an unexpected tropical storm (*surazo*) swept in, dropping the temperature by twenty-five to thirty degrees, and turning our tropical escapade into a freezer-on-wheels experience. Alan gave me his only jacket and draped a bright yellow plastic poncho over me while he and Larry, our two brave captains, faced the storm head-on. They took turns steering, navigating through deep ruts of mud and water as the wind and rain played percussion on their backs.

I swayed back and forth in my seat inside the trailer as the rain poured down and the floods came up—my bright yellow poncho, the only splash of color in a sea of muddy brown. The boat-like trailer left me sitting in a pool of water splashing at my oversized black rubber boots. I could see this was going to be a *very long* trip!

Once we left the jungle portion of the road, local Bolivians, guardians of the improved portion of the logging road, had put up roadblocks and weren't keen at all about our swamp tractor turning their track into an even muddier playground. After Alan and Larry assured them that the buggy's huge tires were gentle giants, their hearts softened, and we were given the green light.

A local lady, wanting to give my head added protection from the pouring rain, ran into her jungle hut to get a straw hat. She returned not only with a holey straw hat but also with a bunch of large green leaves clenched in her fist. Declaring the leaves had medicinal powers, she proceeded to plaster them over my engorged cheek. Then, observing me sympathetically, she crowned my already hooded yellow plastic head with the large, holey straw hat. It was all she could do to help. There I was, a mix of yellow plastic and broken straw with green leaves plastered on my engorged cheek.

As I stood in the pouring rain in all my dripping glory, the yellow hood drooping over my puffy face, I peeked out from under the leafy green compress to catch sight of Alan and Larry through the squint of my swollen eye. Casting me sympathetic smiles, they mustered all their forces to restrain from chuckling. I was quite the spectacle to behold. At least I was dry and felt no pain in my jaw, thanks to a God who heard and answered our prayers. The guys helped me into the seat at the back of the trailer, which by then had turned into a makeshift pool, and we set off again. As they bravely navigated the swampy terrain, I bid farewell to our gracious host and prepared for the soggy, swaying ride.

Our journey turned into an impressive saga of jostling and jolting, with the trailer serving as a boat on the choppy sea of mud. Clutching my seat for dear life, I watched as the swamp buggy swam its way through flooded areas with its massive tires keeping us afloat. Thirteen hours of this aquatic rodeo left me feeling very weary, but we finally made it to the graveled road leading to Santa Cruz. With the day nearly done and no buses in sight, it appeared we had no choice but to trundle the rest of the way to Santa Cruz aboard our trusty swamp steed, at a pace that would make most turtles scoff.

In God's tender mercies, He had already drafted a superior plan for this road-weary band, particularly for the pregnant mother draped in yellow sitting in back. Our colleague, Larry, just "happened" to see a sawmill proprietor, an acquaintance of his, who just "happened" to be hopping into his truck at his sawmill. In a stroke of God's providential care, Mr. Cuellar offered us a ride for a good seventy kilometers along the gravel road to his other lumber operation. We bid adieu to our swampland chariot at his mill and boarded his pickup.

En route, Alan and Larry seized the opportunity to share the Gospel with Mr. Cuellar, a man who professed to be unacquainted with the wonderful story of Jesus. Moved by the narrative and my plight, as we approached his second sawmill, he generously proposed to extend our journey to Santa Cruz that very night. He had errands to do there the next day. Once again, our merciful God had gone before, making a way for his weary servants.

Throughout that arduous journey of fifteen hours, the persistent pain in my jaw was barely noticeable only for it to surge back as we neared the mission guest home in the final half-hour. It was evident that the Lord had eased my suffering during the most challenging part of our trip. *Isaiah 27:8 KJV He stays His rough wind in the day of His east wind.* This verse speaks to the notion that God softens adversity to match the endurance of those who are suffering, ensuring their afflictions do not exceed their capacity to bear them. God had removed my pain for all but the last thirty minutes of our trip.

What we anticipated as a brief stay in Santa Cruz unexpectedly stretched into two full weeks. The infection had entrenched itself so deeply in my jaw that a ten-day regimen of potent antibiotic injections was necessary before any dental work could begin. Although the accommodations at the Santa Cruz mission guest house were comfortable, being away from our two young children weighed heavily on my heart, even though I knew they were in the capable hands of our colleagues back at the Víbora camp.

Once the antibiotics took care of the infection, attention could finally be turned to my troublesome tooth. We have wondered if the intensive application of antibiotics may have contributed to enduring health issues our youngest son Caleb faces to this day. He was developing in my womb at that time, and the drugs had to have a negative impact on his forming body. Though this saddens us, we acknowledge that, given the circumstances, we had no other alternatives at the time.

The Pink Flamingo

During the two weeks in Santa Cruz attending to my tooth, God made available to our team a robust, diesel-fueled swamp tractor. This new purchase, shared with our coworkers, was essential to our contact work. With the helicopter out of service, our two sturdy swamp tractors became our main mode of transportation through the dense jungle. We thanked God for providing these formidable vehicles.

Nevertheless, I was not looking forward to our return trip back through the jungle, though the thought of reuniting with our children spurred me on. Our newer blue swamp tractor trundled at about a quarter of the pace of a regular vehicle, so we spent the majority of the first day traveling the paved road out of Santa Cruz. Evening was approaching and we needed to accommodate pup tents at the edge of the forest near the side of the road before tackling the 12–13-hour trek through the jungle. The public road was not heavily traveled, though heavy trucks occasionally would rumble past, heading towards Santa Cruz with cargo.

The guys set up the tents in a sandy patch near the road. Alan played MacGyver with the tractor, yanking off every last cushion it had so he could make the ground softer for his pregnant wife. He was well aware that I had a touch of the "princess and the pea" syndrome when it came to getting a good night's rest. Finally, my Sir Galahad shed his only jacket to add to the cushioning before laying out the one and only sleeping bag on top.

After I crawled into my makeshift bed, Alan lay down next to me with nothing but the bare tent floor beneath him—no pillow, no blanket, no jacket—nothing except his clothing! "You're not going to sleep on the bare tent floor, are you?" I exclaimed. "You won't sleep a wink!" "Oh yes I will!" he shot back.

We joined hands in prayer before retiring. Our tents were tucked as far away from the road as the encroaching jungle would allow. In this land of no speed limits, Alan's concern about speeding trucks passing by unawares was not unfounded. He committed our safety to the Lord in prayer, then closed his eyes. Before I had time to adjust my sleeping bag, he was snoring a gentle lullaby at my side. I gazed over at his dead-to-the-world expression, marveling; that man could sleep anywhere!

As for me, falling asleep was hopeless. I flipped and flopped, seeking comfort in vain on the uneven ground, my discomfort only punctuated by envious glances at my slumbering hero. His sleep seemed unshakable. Despite closing my eyes, I remained alert to every sound throughout the night.

Around 2:00 a.m., the thundering roar of a large truck engine could be heard at a distance, its headlights slicing through the darkness. I remained calm, knowing by the light trajectory that we were safe, but the truck's thunderous approach catapulted Alan into full-blown *escape danger at all costs* mode! He shot up like a jack-in-the-box and anxiously flailed at our tent's rear wall, scrambling to get out and alert the driver with wild arm-waving. His goal; to signal the driver of our roadside encampment.

In his groggy panic-stricken state, he battled the back of the tent instead of the front. No wonder the door eluded him! "Alan, there's plenty of room for the truck to clear our tent," I hollered over the engine's roar. "Besides, you're at the back of the tent, not the front!"

With perception kicking in, he made it to the front of the pup tent and found the door. By that time though, the truck had already whizzed by. It only took a few seconds for him to compose himself; then, without a word, he lay back down on the stark tent floor and within a minute, that man was back into a deep sleep! Astonishing! I fitfully tossed and turned throughout the rest of the night until the first rays of sunlight pierced through our tent, heralding the arrival of a new dawn.

After packing up, we embarked once again on our swamp tractor journey through the rainforest. Clear, blue skies had dried up the logging track but left deep ruts on the makeshift road. After about six hours of the jarring trek, I felt utterly drained. Knowing we had another six or seven hours of travel ahead before reaching the Víbora camp, my spirits sank. We were only halfway home.

Our Heavenly Father, who daily showers His children with tender mercies, knew exactly what his child needed to distract her from the wear and fatigue of that moment. It's rare to encounter a pink flamingo in the dense Amazonian wilds, but suddenly, an elegant pink flamingo flew right out of the jungle in front of us as if it were leading the way through the clearing. Encountering one of these Andean flamingos in the jungle (a species so scarce, less than 40,000 of them are said to remain) was truly rare. Only the tender compassion of a Heavenly Father would have led that beautiful bird to fly right in front of his weary, disheartened daughter. I knew that stunning creature was a gift from above the moment it appeared.

The elegant, feathered flamingo unfurled its broad pink wings and glided effortlessly through the cleared trackway as if it were flaunting all its' loveliness. Rain had removed the dust and dirt from the emerald foliage, making a glorious backdrop for the rosy creature as it gracefully glided in front, rounding every bend as if leading the way. For over an hour, the flamingo soared in front of us, lifting my spirits with it. An old hymn, "Wings of a Dove," came to mind, compelling me to break into a soft melody. I swayed through the jungle, serenading the wilderness as we made our way home.

WINGS OF A DOVE
When troubles surround us, when evils come,
The body grows weak
The spirit grows numb
When these things beset us, He doesn't forget us
He sends down His love
On the wings of a dove.

(Written by Bob Ferguson)

Only this time, God sent His pure sweet love on the wings of a Pink Flamingo.

It is of the LORD's mercies that we are not consumed,
Because his compassions fail not.
They are new every morning: Great is thy faithfulness.
Lamentation 3:22–23 KJV

A Perilous Decision

"I just can't shake the feeling that it's too dangerous," I expressed to my husband, worry evident in my voice. "I really don't think you should go." It was now September 1980, and for two years we had made our home at the Víbora River base. Initially, the nomads frequently took gifts from the racks, even venturing to within just a few hundred yards of our camp. However, their visits had become very scarce, and when they did take gifts, it was from the racks three kilometers away.

Previously, when the missionaries were gone from camp, the nomads had entered and stolen machetes. Were they fearful we would retaliate if they came too close? Was this the reason they were keeping their distance?

After discussion and prayer among the contact team and with mission leadership, our men felt they should go looking for the Yuquí to assure them of our friendship and good will towards them. It would be a dangerous effort in the dense rainforest, as the nomads could easily fire arrows at them from ambush. Nevertheless, they decided that having four Yuquí believers from the Chimoré base accompany three of the American missionaries would work well on such an endeavor.

Yuquí with bleeder tipped arrow

I was not happy about this probable plan and prayed earnestly that God would prevent my husband from going. When Alan received an unexpected letter from his father and read it to me, I was certain God had answered my prayers. Surely his dad's advice would convince him not to go.

In the letter, his father cited a passage from Acts 21:11–13. It recounted the prophet Agabus's stark warnings to the Apostle Paul, attempting to dissuade him from traveling to Jerusalem due to the imminent dangers he would face there. Interpreting these verses as a clear caution from God, his dad expressed grave concern and strongly urged his son not to go. My sentiments exactly!

> *Acts 21:11–12 NIV Coming over to us, he took Paul's belt, tied his own hands and feet with it and said, "The Holy Spirit says, 'In this way the Jewish leaders in Jerusalem will bind the owner of this belt and will hand him over to the Gentiles.'" When we heard this, we and the people there pleaded with Paul not to go up to Jerusalem.*

What more needed to be said? Alan had a great respect for his dad and it was clear his father had the same premonitions that I did about the projected plan. It was just too dangerous!

Remarkably, and with a surprising twist, God had led Alan to exactly the same verses while he sought the Lord's will about the matter. He had been meditating on Acts 21:11–13 even before his dad's letter arrived. To my astonishment, it was not the warnings about the danger that resonated with my husband, but rather Paul's courageous response in verse 13!

> *Then Paul answered, what mean ye to weep and to break my heart? For I am ready not to be bound only, but also to die at Jerusalem for the name of the Lord Jesus. Acts 21:13 KJV*

This was *not* what I wanted to hear! My heart sank when Alan shared how the Lord spoke so clearly to him through those verses.

Nevertheless, I had resolved beforehand not to stand in the way of God's will if he was meant to go. Consequently, a team consisting of four Yuquí believers and three American missionaries got ready to leave. Let me fill you in on some of the details of this endeavor adapted from the narratives in my husband's book.

The team left the Víbora River base following the gift trail leading out to the jungle. Eventually, they made it to an oil drilling site where they picked up some valuable information from a woodsman who reportedly knew the area well. He had seen numerous signs of the hostiles. The woodsman graciously hosted the American and Yuquí missionaries in his modest, dirt-floored, thatch-roofed house without walls. A cold, wet storm had moved in so our guys were grateful for what would be their last night with a shelter over their heads.

Straight Hair on the far right in the early days

The next day, they picked up some semi-fresh Yuquí trails, so one of the Yuquí guides, Wooly Hair, along with his brother Straight Hair, led the way. Both were outstanding trackers. This was the fourth day of their expedition and even though they carried guns, living off the land was difficult, so they were grateful for the modest amount of dry food they had carried.

With the weather cold and drizzly, the team stopped occasionally to light a fire just to get warm. One of his Yuquí friends remarked: "*Tata amama ta yegua.*" (I'll huddle around the fire and warm myself.) Alan remembered those words for future use as well as many other Yuquí phrases.

Early the next morning the crew headed out again and the farther into the unknown they ventured, the fresher the signs of the nomads

Straight Hair while helping us at the Víbora

became. Fear intensified in the Chimoré Yuquí as they realized contact could be imminent and the hostiles might spot them at any time. The Christian Yuquí were all too familiar with the mindset of their unfriendly relatives and the magnitude of risk they were taking. It had only been fifteen years earlier that they were the ones piercing the *abaa* (the enemy outsiders) with their bleeder tipped arrows.

The rainforest was so dense with overgrown vines that moving forward required strenuous cutting with a machete, so the men took turns chopping their way through the woods. By 4:30 p.m., they were exhausted, so stopped to camp for the night. It had rained throughout the day and although they stopped often to huddle under a tarp during the heaviest downpours until the rain lightened, all of them were soaked to the skin. A camp fire would help warm them before they crawled into their mosquito nets for the night.

The following day, they arrived at the Chore River which was swollen with water due to so much rain. Since the Yuquí guides didn't know how to swim, they needed help crossing in the swift current. Eventually all the men were safely on the other side. Just a few yards further into the jungle, they came upon a dead *capybara* (the world's largest rodent). This left them perplexed as the only things missing from the carcass was its head and hide.

Further on they stumbled upon a large, abandoned camp near the river with four main fires. It was surrounded by long walls of palm branches which provided protection and concealment from the outside. In the camp was a *capybara* skull, a howler monkey jawbone, blue macaw feathers, a turtle skeleton, and assorted other camp debris. "Very likely, a high-class individual died, and the people aren't eating capybara meat since it was the deceased person's favorite meat in life," the Yuquí guides alerted the team.

Everyone knew the implications of a high-class Yuquí dying and it wasn't reassuring! This meant the hostile nomads would need more than one victim to kill in order to accompany the deceased Yuquí's spirit in the afterlife. Our men could be potential targets.

A few days prior to this, a thorn-covered sapling had sprung back as my husband was hiking the trail and embedded a thorn deep into his knee. The barb was embedded so deeply that it was impossible to extract. During the next two days, his knee became very infected and swollen, making it extremely difficult for Alan to walk. The crew stopped for a while so he could rest and soak his knee in saltwater hoping it would draw the thorn out. Meanwhile, some of the Yuquí guides scouted the surrounding area. They found yet another camp but could not determine which direction the jungle nomads had traveled from there.

Alan's knee remained so swollen and painful that Big Tummy, one of the Yuquí guides, stayed to tend to him while the other five men scouted the area north of them. By the time the squad returned, Alan's knee had stiffened up considerably and it was doubtful he would be able to walk the next day. No firewood was seen in the last abandoned camp which likely indicated the nomads had only traveled a short distance from there and took the firewood with them to their next campsite. It frustrated my husband knowing contact with the *Bia* was imminent. Here they were, so close, and he was unable to walk any further.

The fellas made camp that evening. Although much of the infection from the knee had drained throughout the night, it only grew stiffer, making it sheer agony for Alan to walk. The next day, he courageously trudged onward, walking last so as not to slow the others. As hard as he tried, he just couldn't keep up and eventually was forced to halt. By this time, the Yuquí guides were dragging their feet as well knowing their good friend and comrade could continue no further. Food supplies were dwindling as well as their desire to encounter their violent jungle kinfolk.

With contact so imminent, the team couldn't abandon the effort now! After seeking the Lord's guidance, they came up with a new strategy. A military helicopter would be called to pick up Bob Garland from the Chimoré base and replace Alan. Having many years of experience working with the Yuquí at the Chimoré, Bob spoke the Yuquí dialect and, like my husband, was loved and respected by the Yuquí. Bob could also resupply them with food stuffs which would raise the morale of the Yuquí guides. Though everyone hated to see their comrade leave, they knew there was no sense in Alan continuing until he got medical attention.

Bob Garland with Chief at the Chimoré base

A large Huey, (utility military helicopter), picked up Bob Garland along with additional supplies at the Chimoré base and arrived at the tiny beach on the Chore River where Alan was waiting. The men had clearly communicated that the helicopter should be loaded as lightly as possible as this was a "hot stop," which required hovering over water and a tiny beach surrounded by trees.

Unfortunately, the word never seemed to reach those manning the aircraft. Two other pilots were on board and as the pilot flying the chopper flew over the small beach and saw the overhanging jungle trees at the river's edge, he considered just aborting the whole procedure. At the last moment, he had second thoughts and decided to make a go of it. While he hovered between the shore and river, Bob threw supplies out onto the small beach and hopped out while Alan painfully crawled aboard. Soon the Huey was in the air heading toward the eastern range of the towering Andes Mountains on their way to Cochabamba. They had a long trip, fraught with bad weather and lengthy delays which are all detailed in my husband's book. After numerous setbacks, Alan finally arrived at the mission guest house where his good friend, Cam Hurst, graciously helped him clean up and get settled for the night.

Crushing News

The doctor arrived the following day. After prescribing Gentamicin injections and limited walking, the medic was out the door. This was good news to my husband, but even better news arrived by radio that afternoon. The missionaries had made contact with the nomads in the jungle and were interacting with them at that very moment!

The team had a friendly two-hour encounter with seven Yuquí warriors, three women, and three children. At first, the jungle nomads were apprehensive, but after about fifteen to twenty minutes of conversation with the Yuquí believers from the Chimoré base, they recognized our team was friendly and meant no harm. Instead, they realized our men were there to protect them. The group was given a variety of gifts including hard candy and bananas, these being gifts they had previously taken from our gift racks, and their dull machetes were sharpened. The Yuquí believers encouraged them to come to our Víbora base where more gifts awaited them. Everything appeared to be so very promising!

Unbeknownst to all of us though, an invisible celestial war was raging in the unseen world.

Be sober, be vigilant; because your adversary
the devil walks about like a roaring lion, seeking
whom he may devour. 1 Peter 5:8 NKJV

For our struggle is not against flesh and blood, but
against the rulers, against the authorities, against the
powers of this dark world and against the spiritual forces
of evil in the heavenly realms. Ephesians 6:12 NIV

. . . .

As evening approached, the missionary crew pulled back to set up camp for the night. They were elated with how well the contact had gone and agreed to return to the nomad's camp the following day. Being extremely exhausted, the men opted to skip supper and get the mosquito nets set up so they could get some much-needed sleep. All of them slept directly on the ground under heavy, white gauze mosquito nets. This made it difficult to see into the nets from the outside; however, from inside their nets, the men could see out. By 10:30 p.m. most of the team was fast asleep.

Crushing news greeted Alan the following morning. During the night, by the light of a full moon, the Yuquí warriors had surrounded our sleeping men and fired arrows randomly into their mosquito nets. Our Víbora comrade and next-door neighbor, Wallace Pouncy, saw the warriors' shadowy forms just moments before they shot. As he was grabbing his gun to fire into the air to frighten them away, a large bleeder tipped arrow impacted him, piercing his thigh.

Two of the Yuquí guides from the Chimoré were also shot. One was losing a lot of blood; his leg had also been pierced by a bleeder tipped arrow. The sharp tips measure twelve to fifteen inches long and two to three inches wide and the wide curve of the bamboo can easily cause the victim to bleed to death. The other Yuquí guide was struck with a barbed arrow so was not as critically wounded.

For some divine reason, God had allowed the hostiles to shoot, but that didn't mean He was not watching over our men. The heavily gauzed mosquito nets prevented the hostiles from discerning our men's forms and the arrows intended to pierce their chests impacted their legs instead. Four arrows were shot and three of our men were badly wounded. The fourth arrow landed just twelve inches from the head of Larry Depue. God had protected all of them from certain death.

Why had the nomads attacked when they had demonstrated such friendship the previous afternoon? We couldn't understand why and wouldn't recognize their reason until much later. The nomads desperately longed for our friendship, our many gifts, and the protection we were offering them; but Satan's lies had convinced them another matter was far more urgent.

Fellow missionaries in the cities of Cochabamba and Santa Cruz urgently searched for any helicopter available to get the men evacuated from the jungle but no military helicopters were available. Eventually a different chopper was found, and the men were airlifted to the Chimoré base, home to Bob Garland and the three Yuquí believers. After three flights and almost six hours, the evacuation was completed. Dark ominous clouds were closing in by then and threatened rain. God held back the storm long enough to get all the men to the Chimoré. From there our mission pilot, Chuck Henson, flew the three wounded men to Cochabamba and by late afternoon, they were in the hospital receiving medical attention.

With no airstrip at the Víbora base at that time, Larry Depue had to make the rigorous trip through the jungle back to our Víbora camp to oversee things there. Two single men had been left in charge while our husbands were away.

The shooting incident shook my husband up much more than he cared to admit. As a single missionary, death had held little fear for him, but now that he had a wife and young children, the thought of leaving them all alone sobered him greatly. He began to doubt the nomads would ever come out to us on their own, especially after this. It seemed there was nothing strong enough to lure the jungle band into our camp at the Vibora.

★★★★★★★★

Terror By Night

Courage is being scared to death—
and saddling up anyway.
John Wayne

After a long harrowing night helping his wounded comrades, Larry Depue made the rigorous trip through the jungle and arrived safely back at our Víbora base. God had spared his life during the ambush when a large Yuquí arrow missed piercing his head by a mere twelve inches. Because Alan was getting medical treatment in the city, Larry made his way to our jungle house to check on me and the children. I was pregnant with our third child at the time.

Our abode was located at the far end of camp next to a clearing of 100 yards before reaching the jungle. The gift rack stood in full view. Just beyond it, a gift trail had been cleared that extended into the shrouded jungle.

"I don't want to frighten you in any way," Larry stated, "but we need to be on high alert here in camp. The ambush has left us shorthanded and the Yuquí know that."

Two single missionary men had remained with the wives and children to oversee things in camp while the other men were in the bush searching for the nomads. With Larry's arrival, we now had three able bodied men in camp. Larry's wife and children, me and our children, and Wallace Pouncy's wife, Barbara, completed the group.

"The nomads are afraid to go out in the dark, but with the full moon shining so brightly, there's the chance they may return with malicious intent. We need to remain very alert and take every precaution we can. You and the children are welcome to stay at our house if you'd like," Larry continued.

With four young children and a wife, Larry's household was full, and I knew space was limited. Having navigated a rough trip through the jungle right after the harrowing ordeal of the ambush only underscored the stress of the situation. Now the weight of managing responsibilities at our Víbora camp rested heavily upon his shoulders.

The sun shone brightly in the blue sky and I hardly had time to process all the bad news. Our good friend Barbara Pouncy, a dear mentor to me, lived right next door to us. Surely the children and I could just stay with her, or so I imagined. My biggest concern at the moment was not to add any extra burdens on Larry.

"I think I can tough it out Larry," I responded, fully regretting later on that I had refused his offer.

"Are you sure?" he asked with concern.

"Yes, I'm sure."

"I brought a gun over for you and need to show you how to use it. I want you to keep it locked and close at hand at all times. If you need me for any reason, shoot it into the air," he instructed.

It hadn't even occurred to me that my friend Barbara would want to join her husband, Wallace, in the city. Duh! He had been pierced in the thigh with a bleeder-tipped arrow. Though I recognized she needed to be by her husband's side, it was with a heavy heart that I bid farewell to her later that morning as she climbed aboard our swamp tractor. One of the single men waited at the wheel.

Being several years my senior and a source of strength and encouragement to me, the lack of Barbara's presence hit me hard.

After climbing aboard the blue swamp tractor, she waved good-bye as they took off using the same logging track I had traveled with my abscessed tooth. Once they arrived in the city of Santa Cruz, Barbara would catch a flight to Cochabamba where she could join her husband while he convalesced in the hospital there.

This meant the Pouncy's house right next door to ours stood totally vacant. Larry and Linda's place was on the other side of Barbara's house, and beyond that was the place where the single fellas were staying. Events happened with such rapidity that every one of us struggled to process the comings and goings. As I look back now, I would have handled things differently, but hindsight is always clearer than foresight. The situation we found ourselves in was a learning curve for all of us.

Throughout that day, I feigned things were normal and kept our two toddlers busy inside. I didn't want them to sense anything was amiss. It was much easier though, hiding my trepidations during the daylit hours; when darkness fell over our jungle base, it was a different story altogether.

As the golden moon climbed the night sky in all its glowing splendor, terror gripped my heart like it had never gripped it before. "The Yuquí are afraid to go out in the dark, but with the full moon shining so brightly, there's the chance of them returning with malicious intent." Larry's words chilled me.

The sun setting over the jungle

I yanked the blue cotton curtains shut and lit the kerosene pressure lamp. What if armed Yuquí warriors were lurking in the woods just beyond our clearing? They could easily spot our silhouettes in the glow of the pressure lamp. I hurried to get the children fed and put to bed early. I *had* to extinguish that lamp!

Once settled in their beds, I read our two toddlers their favorite story book, hoping they wouldn't notice the trembling in my hands. After that, we each took turns praying, as was our nightly routine. "Please dear God, fix Daddy's leg so he can come back home soon," one of the children entreated. Never had I so acutely sensed my husband's absence.

Yuquí warriors

Finishing with hugs and kisses, I tucked in their mosquito nets; then, hurried to grab a flashlight and Bible before extinguishing the pressure lamp in our kitchen/living area. After setting the gun close to our bed, I leapt under the mosquito net unwashed, unfed, and uncomforted, with adrenaline pumping madly through my veins.

The full moon's light glowed through our bedroom curtains and I trembled uncontrollably. Grabbing my Bible and flashlight, I hid under the covers, then turned to the only One who could calm the terror raging in my breast. *Lord, you've promised never to leave me or forsake me. Please calm the gripping fear that is overwhelming me.* Beneath the covers and with the aid of a flashlight, I searched through my Bible Concordance for any verses addressing fear.

Do not be afraid of sudden terror, for the Lord will be your confidence. Proverbs 3:25–26 ESV

He will cover you with his feathers. He will shelter you with his wings. His faithful promises are your armor and protection. Do not be afraid of the terrors of the night, nor the arrow that flies in the day .Psalm 91:4–5 NLT

Even though I walk through the valley of the shadow of death, I will fear no evil, for You are with me... Psalm 23:4 ESV

"You are with me...You are with me." I repeated those words over and over until the truth began to sink in. Not only was the Lord right there with me, but His presence was living inside my heart. Slowly, His promises comforted my trembling heart and in the wee hours of the morning, I fell asleep.

> I will both lie down and sleep; for You alone,
> O Lord, make me dwell in safety. Psalm 4:8 NKJV

Alan's knee had finally healed sufficiently to make the long trip inland to the Víbora base. During his absence, God graciously gave me the fortitude and courage to face things on my own, but oh, what a reassuring comfort it was to wrap my arms around my husband when he returned.

With Alan back in camp, the Larry Depue family left for the city to recuperate from the trauma of the ambush. Wallace Pouncy was convalescing in Cochabamba with Barbara by his side which left only our small family and one single man, Lonnie Hodge, remaining at the base to keep an eye on things. As soon as the other two families returned, the contact team would reevaluate and decide if we should abandon efforts at the Víbora base.

Fishing and hunting trips were too dangerous to be made. Our supply of frozen meat in the little gas-powered fridge was nil and we were living on dried beans, rice, and bananas from our crops. The fare was beginning to get old. The only safe place to walk outside was on the banks of the Víbora River flowing just beyond our houses. Because the Yuquí couldn't swim, we were safe walking on the stretch between the houses and the river.

Early one morning, Alan was walking along the river edge in front of our house when he turned and stealthily crept into the house. "There's a large surubí (a tiger-striped catfish that tastes delicious) sunning itself by the bank," he whispered. Grabbing his bow and arrows, he dashed back out the door. I watched as he tiptoed to the river's edge where he poised himself to take aim. With perfect precision, he lodged the arrow right in the center of the fish's body. A heavy string was attached to the arrow with a sealed plastic bottle at the end designed to float. The large 20-pound *surubí* thrashed and battered the water while Alan ran to get Lonnie Hodge's help. With the aid of the canoe, they located the bottle bobbing up and down and retrieved the big fish. How grateful we were to dine on such a delicacy that night and once again have a full freezer. Just as God had provided meat for Elijah in the wilderness, so He provided meat for us within the small confines of our jungle camp.

The ravens brought him bread and meat in the morning and bread and meat in the evening, and he drank from the brook. 1 Kings 17:6 NKJV

Alan and Vickie with surubí and pacú

A Welcome Return

For the next two years, the contact base on the Víbora River lay totally abandoned; the missionaries there disbanded to help out with other ministries around Bolivia. This gave all of us a hiatus to recover from the trauma of the shootings, not to mention time for the hostile nomads to cool off. Alan and I returned to the Chimoré River base where once again, I put on my nurse's cap. By this time, we had three young children; our youngest son Caleb was about eight months old.

Chief with Les Foster in the early days

It was a welcome change for us to actually be working with this settled group of Yuquí once again. After three years of waiting at the Víbora camp for opportunities to make contact with the hostile Yuquí, we welcomed the chance to be working with the advanced group at the Chimoré base.

Alan's parents, Les and Lois Foster, along with their colleagues, had established a friendly relationship with the first band of Yuquí people at this base in 1965.

When we arrived, having departed from the Víbora area, it was a tremendous honor to work alongside Bob and Mary Garland who had a deep understanding of the Yuquí culture and language due to their work with Alan's folks.

Bob and Mary Garland

Bob, known for his engaging wit and delightful sense of humor, oversaw the work there and regularly taught Bible lessons in the Yuquí dialect. Meanwhile, Mary, a skilled linguist, played a pivotal role in translating the New Testament into Yuquí and compiled an extensive grammar guide and dictionary for the language.

Dick Strickler, the other veteran member of the team, worked in the area of literacy, and taught a few of the more promising adults to read. This was a trying task, but a necessary one if the translated New Testament was to be put to good use. The leaders in the developing church needed to be able to study the Word of God on their own. A Bolivian family, Mariano and Leonarda Ichu, who worked alongside us, taught the Yuquí children attending the school at the base. Through their contact with Mariano and his family, the younger Yuquí were becoming bilingual, learning Spanish, which is the principal language of Bolivia.

Our home at the Chimoré base was a roomy, two-level timber structure that comfortably accommodated our family of five. The upper-level housed bedrooms while the lower level featured a living room, small study, and kitchen. The two-floor design ensured that the ground floor remained cooler during the warmest parts of the day. Conveniently, the clinic was close and easy to access.

The nearby clinic, Sammy at the door

Younger Yuquí families and individuals regularly came to visit us in the evenings. They were eager to listen to cassette tapes, enjoying music or narratives in Spanish, which helped them improve their skills in this new language. Meanwhile, Alan studied the Yuquí language in his office nearby. Our children found real joy interacting with our guests, particularly on several evenings when a Yuquí girl introduced a brood of baby armadillos to our home. How delightful it was to watch the creatures roll themselves up into little balls on our concrete floor and then unfurl to lap milk from a dish. The Yuquí were like family to us, and spending the evenings with them was something we enjoyed and cherished.

One of the teenage girls, Susanna, became a close friend of mine and regularly assisted me in taking our children to the beach. The riverbank, with its soft sand and shallow waters, provided endless entertainment for our children. On one occasion, as we made our way to the river, Susanna cautioned me about biting snails—a warning I pieced together from her fragmented Spanish and my limited understanding of Yuquí.

Biting snails? I couldn't imagine a snail biting someone, but I soon learned it was true. Unbeknownst to me, our one-year-old son Caleb innocently picked up a snail while playing in the sand. The slimy creature slipped into its shell and swiftly shut the shell door firmly behind, taking a chunk of Caleb's tender thumb with it. The incident caused our toddler considerable pain and distressed me greatly. How sorry I was that I hadn't been more vigilant watching out for those "biting" snails! Fortunately, Caleb's thumb recovered after two weeks, with an unexpected benefit emerging from the whole ordeal. The bite helped curb his thumb-sucking habit, a result we had hoped for but not in such an unfortunate way.

Occasionally, the children and I joined the believers under the shade of a bamboo structure for a time of worship, singing, and Bible teaching in their language. Alan had some basic skills at playing the guitar as well as a pleasant voice. You would have thought John Denver was leading the chorus by the people's response. They absolutely loved it!

We sang a collection of Yuquí choruses put together by Mary Garland, the missionaries singing *especially* loud in our attempts to steer the people to the right musical pitches and tempo. It was hopeless! The closest thing to melodies the Yuquí had ever sung in their nomadic wanderings was wailing and chanting to the spirits of their dead. Even our revered leader, Bob Garland, couldn't carry a tune. Nevertheless, our dear jungle friends sang their hearts out, making a joyful noise to the Lord with "John Denver" at the front singing and strumming his guitar.

Listening to a Bible lesson

Bob usually taught Bible lessons in their dialect with the assistance of key Yuquí believers who also shared insights into the Scriptures. Alan was a regular at these gatherings, contributing to the teachings when possible. As his proficiency in the language increased, he assisted in the Bible teaching more and more. He devoted every spare minute he had to studying the Yuquí language and his efforts were evident.

Beloved Yuquí children

Alan's primary responsibility at the Chimoré base involved the upkeep of the airstrip which, in itself, was a huge responsibility. Vegetation grows at a prodigious rate year-round in the tropics so the arduous work of maintaining the camp and airstrip in the intense heat was both physically demanding and time intensive. He enlisted the help of some Yuquí individuals which took additional time. They usually spent their wages at our small base canteen, particularly on sweetened condensed milk, which was their all-time favorite, or on bullets for the guns they had learned to use.

We cherished our time at the Chimoré base, embracing both the joys of the people as well as their griefs, which were many. My affection for them deepened significantly during our stay, and the memories we created together are indelibly etched in my heart.

The Bloodbath

Field leadership asked us to continue at the Chimoré base for an indefinite period of time, which we were happy to do. It presented us with further opportunities for language acquisition, cultural immersion, and interactions with the settled Yuquí, all of which would be beneficial in building relationships with other Yuquí bands. Meanwhile, a new missionary team at the Víbora base was making strides toward establishing connections with that group of hostile Yuquí. The time arrived for the Garlands to depart for a much-needed furlough in the U.S. which left just Alan, Dick Strickler, and me overseeing affairs at the Chimoré base once again.

I was growing proficient in handling the medical work, even assisting Yuquí women giving birth, yet there remained a singular challenge I fervently wished to avoid at all costs—particularly if I had to handle it alone—a snakebite encounter. The jungle had plenty of pit vipers slithering around and though we continually urged the people to wear shoes for protection, few of them heeded our advice.

Dick Strickler teaching school

One day, a disturbance erupted in the distance that escalated rapidly and a group of Yuquí rushed frantically toward our house. With Alan away, I braced for an emergency. Amidst the chaos, one of the people ran over to tell me that Carolina, a revered older Yuquí lady, had been bitten on the foot by a pit viper. The Yuquí informer reported *"Erucuidn!"* (there is lots and lots of blood), the exact opposite of what I needed to hear to boost my burgeoning medical confidence.

Alarmed, I ran to ask Dick Strickler, the senior missionary in camp, to rush to the clinic and assist me. Soon, another Yuquí arrived, again declaring, *"Erucuidn!"* My knees grew weak. Why did Alan have to be out of camp on *this* particular morning? More people gathered, bringing additional reports of gloom and doom and repeated declarations of, *"Erucuidn."* Unbeknownst to me, the Yuquís' worst fear was snake bite, and *all* snake bites were critical in their estimation. This terror always hyped them into declaring there was "lots and lots of blood."

At a distance I spotted a Yuquí man cradling an elderly woman; the woman lay limply in his arms. With heart pounding, I hurried to prep the clinic's examination table, bracing for the worst. I peeked outside, hoping to see Dick Strickler on his way. *What could possibly be delaying him?* I wondered.

In the meantime, Dick, back at the canteen shop, insisted on locking up tight to prevent any mischief during his absence. Considering his age and his inclination towards perfectionism, Dick was not one to move quickly. Everything was done with a slow, deliberate, and methodical approach, which meant his arrival at the clinic was not done at breakneck speed.

Meanwhile, the Yuquí man arrived and laid the revered grandma on the examining table. I gazed at her with awe and wonder: she was immaculately bloodless! I couldn't find even a spec of blood on her foot despite their outcries of, *"Erucuidn."* Dick finally reached the clinic clutching an older book, a manual for the medically deserted.

From across the room, he recited its ancient wisdom slowly and deliberately. "It says here to apply a tourniquet first, then use the blade to cut an X-mark incision."

I gazed at the grubby foot; the silence was heavy.

He droned on with the instructions: "Then suck the venom out of the wound, spit, and repeat." Oh, the joy of knowing I'd be the one playing vampire and not Dick! The manual was our trusty go-to. Our antivenom stash was in the refrigerator stored away for critical cases.

"Hold on just a minute Dick!" His monologue was cut short as I seized a magnifying glass. I inspected the alleged bite, magnified to a landscape of skin folds and dirt deposits, searching for a speck of blood. I searched and searched for just a pinpoint of the red, life-sustaining plasma that the Yuquí had claimed there was "lots and lots of." There was nary a speck. Nor could I find any evidence of a fang mark; this was less a snake bite and more a mystery swathed in a dirty foot.

I washed Carolina's foot with soap and water and examined again for any clue that the snake fangs had actually penetrated her skin. Zilch, Zippo, Nada! After some discussion, Dick and I decided on the best course of action: elevate, ice, and monitor. So, for several hours I played sentry. She was as good as new when she finally toddled off home. That evening, Alan and I laughed as I recounted the "bloodbath" the Yuquí had declared took place, and my less dramatic findings. Though we chuckled over the incident, we were extremely

Carolina

grateful it had been a false alarm. Little did we know that fate had a cruel twist in store, with a tiny pit viper that would soon cast a long, dark shadow over all of our spirits at the Chimoré base.

★★★★★★★

The Pit Viper

Marina had been harvesting rice in the hot sun, and feeling overly tired, had wanted to rest, but her husband forbade her. Every hand was needed. Even though she was eight months pregnant, there was too much work to be done.

Although it was just a small snake, it lay in ambush for her. As she went about harvesting rice, the moment came when the pit viper launched its attack. Her scream pierced the air as she bolted, only to collapse a short distance away, screaming in terror, "I'm going to die! I'm going to die!" Then she lost consciousness, never to rouse again. Marina was not just a cherished friend of ours but also a precious sister in Christ, having embraced Jesus as her Savior years before.

Paraphrasing from my husband's account regarding this tragic incident:

The people's wails resounded loudly as they proceeded down the airstrip. They were hauling Marina to the clinic in a wheelbarrow. When Alan approached, he asked them why they were all crying so much. Being overcome with so much grief, no one answered. He had no idea that Marina was unconscious and not breathing or he may have tried cardiac massage and mouth-to-mouth resuscitation right then and there; but it was already too late.

There was no coffin; no change of clothing for her. Just as she had been brought from the rice field, they would place her in the ground. Just two-and-a-half hours before, she had been a healthy, expectant mother working in the rice field.

Alan watched somberly as they laid her on the fresh green banana leaves at the bottom of a dark earthen cavity. Then they covered her with dirt. A variety of items were handed to the men standing in the grave—cups, cloth, a knife—things to be buried with her. Her dog and chickens had already been killed. Her mother-in-law took care of that detail before bringing her to us.

The anguished, grief-stricken wails from her husband, Jaime, and mother-in-law disrupted Alan's thoughts. Losing a young wife so suddenly, especially one that was eight months pregnant, had to rip his heart in two. Had her husband thought about his young wife's faith in Christ as her Savior? Would knowing she was in heaven be of any comfort at all to him or were his thoughts related to their cultural beliefs concerning the spirits of the dead? Her young son Juan stood all alone and off to one side. Everyone's sympathy was for Marina's husband, Jaime.

Her death was so unexpected, so sudden! The reality of it hadn't really gripped us until the following day. Jaime, accompanied by some of his family members, arrived at our house early the next morning. He was a close friend to Alan. Ascending the steps to our porch, he entrusted Alan with his shotgun. "Would you keep this for me while I'm gone? I don't want to shoot myself."

Then, overcome with emotion, he wept uncontrollably. Alan embraced him, and they both cried, leaving me standing at the side with tears streaming down my face. In their profound grief, Jaime and his family left and ventured into the jungle's shadows for a few days, taking only essentials. The wilderness offered them some solace, a balm for their shattered spirits. Meanwhile, life continued for those who stayed, as they carried on with the rice harvest.

Critters

Sammy, Becky, Caleb caught playing in the mud

Our two-year tenure at the Chimoré base was a period brimming with happiness, as our children reveled in a variety of engaging activities. One of their favorites was manning the canoe all on their own. After a night of heavy rain, a shallow pool of water covered our yard, leading Alan to fetch a canoe and paddle from the shed before heading to work. From my vantage point at either the kitchen window or porch, I watched over our children's adventures. Four-year-old Sammy immediately took charge handling the operations. By standing in front and shoving a paddle into the grassy ground below, the canoe glided through the crystal-clear waters. Three-year-old Becky vociferously commanded orders from the front seat like a boss while fellow crewman, two-year-old Caleb, sat in back wide-eyed with delight.

The kids also enjoyed wading in the shallow waters at the riverbank and swinging from a tire beneath a shade tree in our yard. They frolicked with their baby goats, and enjoyed watching the *Bia* who constantly transported large catches of fish and game through camp.

Becky, Sammy, and Caleb with their pet goats

Favorite Joven with a jaguar

One day, Favorite Joven returned from a hunting trip and proudly displayed a majestic black and tan-or-ange jaguar he had killed. The demise of such a magnificent creature saddened me, yet for the Yuquí, hunting was a major component of their life; thus, the concept of "endangered species" was not found in their vocabulary.

The fishing was good

The wide-spread diversity of wildlife in the jungle was not only captivating but provided us with a constant source of intrigue. There was the instance where we watched a spectacle that rivaled any scene in Alfred Hitchcock's iconic film "The Birds." At the time, we lived in a roomy two-story house built of concrete block and lumber at the Chimoré base. It didn't take long for us to discover the previous owners had not sealed the area between the roof and ceiling where multitudes of bats had taken up residence. Indeed, some of them may have been vampire bats!

Baby Caleb

Our baby son still nursed through the night, and I was his midnight snack provider. That's when I discovered our upstairs bedrooms offered aerial shows of bats throughout the nocturnal hours. As I hastily shuffled our youngest to our bed for a peaceful feed, I'd often have to dodge a swooping bat. Sprinting across the floor with baby Caleb securely in my arms, I'd dive under the large mosquito net over the master bed where I could nurse him in peace. It wasn't long before Alan turned bat wrangling into an Olympic sport. By swinging a broom through the air, the bat's sound waves became so bamboozled, Alan could whack the "flittermouse" down with a broom and kill it.

The day arrived when enough was enough! Those bats had to go! The children and I watched outside from a distance as Alan waged chemical warfare spraying kerosene into the roof rafters, sending a deluge of disoriented bats into the daylight. The sky grew dark as hundreds of bats, looking like a flurry of miniature black umbrellas, took flight in a frenzied exodus. Thanks to my husband, the space between roof and ceiling was finally cleared and securely sealed, eliminating those "leather flappers" once and for all.

Our two-story lumber house at the Chimoré

Our two-story jungle house also played host to an army of natural pest controllers. Remember the tale of Jill's puppies and the army ants? One day, columns of army ants marched right toward our home on a relentless quest, undeterred by walls or floors. "There's nothing I can do," Alan declared. "We'll just have to leave the house for a few hours and let them do their thing."

Yuquí with cattle rustler bird

It wasn't long before extensive columns of army ants scrambled across the floors and up the walls, filling the house with a living, moving tapestry. We vacated the house and let the six-legged soldiers march on. Their invasion, albeit uninvited, proved to be a blessing in disguise as they swept through the house, evicting every unwelcome cockroach, mouse, or any other living creature in their path. Once their mission was complete, they moved on, allowing us to reclaim our abode. Rest assured, their invasion left us on high alert, watching for any remaining ants.

I'll spare the details of the tadpole of such heft that it tipped the scales at nearly a pound or the harmless caterpillar that perfectly mimicked a poised pit viper ready to strike. Then there was that deceptively charming puss moth caterpillar, robed in lemon-yellow fluff that left a long-lasting and radiating sting on young Sammy's palm, causing me much worry and grief. Alan happened to be on a survey at that time. I could write a whole paragraph about the silent dance of two rare rainbow

A giant armadillo

boas that graced our camp, their colorful iridescence shining in the sun. The Amazon jungle is teeming with incredible life forms, all of which are just another testament to our remarkable Creator who expresses His magnificence through the great diversity of his creations.

★★★★★★★

Disturbing News

While the missionaries relocated and served elsewhere for about two years, the jungle reclaimed our abandoned Víbora outpost, with dense vegetation engulfing the once bustling settlement. We spent the time working with the more advanced group at the Chimoré River base. However, early in 1983, a new missionary team cleared the Víbora site once again and established the base for a second time. During that phase, a jungle airstrip was completed which made access to the Vibora base much less daunting.

With missionaries newly established at the Víbora camp and placing gifts on the racks, the hostiles once again began taking the gifts. Even so, they only removed those toward the end of the trail rather than gifts hanging close to the camp clearing. Clearly, they were reluctant to approach too closely even though large quantities of bananas were growing at our base by that time. The abundance of bananas should have been a big attraction for them but instead, the Yuquí risked their lives stealing bananas from settlers near an abandoned oil exploration site a few kilometers away rather than take the stalks hanging on the gift racks near the missionary camp.

It was around this time we received some very disturbing news. Once again, the nomadic Yuquí were upsetting the colonists and had killed a settler, shooting him full of their formidable arrows. One national hunter described his narrow escape from a previous shooting saying: "You wouldn't believe the force of one of those eight-foot arrows! When the first one hit me in the upper arm, it knocked me straight to the ground, which actually saved my life. Three other arrows flew right over me."

Drawing extensively from my husband's book, I continue...

Due to the latest shooting, the colonists renewed their efforts in calling for the military to annihilate the "savages" once and for all. One attempt had already been made by the armed forces, but rain had hindered their search for the "savages". A government-owned oil company doing exploration in the area had already begun official paperwork to authorize a battalion of soldiers to go in and annihilate the nomadic Yuquí. Missionaries both at the Chimoré and Víbora bases were extremely concerned and began asking God what His plan for them as a missionary team might be.

Back at the Chimoré base, Bob Garland and Alan met with the Christian Yuquí men in camp to discuss the dilemma. Remembering the pain and trauma of the previous ambush, the Yuquí men weren't at all willing to search for their nomadic relatives again, at least not initially.

After being reminded their jungle kin would be completely annihilated without such measures, the Yuquí men had a change of heart. The situation was extremely grave and weighed heavily on both the hearts of the missionaries as well as the Yuquí believers. They sought the Lord earnestly for guidance as to what course of action God would have them take. It was decided that Alan and five of the Yuquí believers, along with their wives, would fly over to join the missionaries at the Víbora camp. Three missionary men, two of whom lived at the Víbora, would join the team, completing the group with nine able bodied men.

Needless to say, after two years of uninterrupted happy family life, I wasn't eager for more separations. Nevertheless, the nomads' lives were at stake, and I would be in good hands at the Chimoré with senior missionaries Bob and Mary Garland living close by.

Five Yuquí families and Alan flew to the Víbora base. After getting settled, the men wasted no time visiting several of the colonist's farms in the area where the shootings had taken place. They gathered as much information as possible.

As the day grew near for the men to head into the jungle in search of the nomads, several of the Christian Yuquí from the Chimoré base got cold feet. My husband's fear was as great as their own, and without complete confidence that God was sending them out, he would not have gone. They gathered together to pray, after which their faith and courage were renewed.

Trekking through the perilous jungle on this particular survey was quite an epic saga that Alan chronicled in his book, *"Someone Must Die."* Navigating in the oppressive heat through the dense steamy jungle was not for the faint hearted. Water and food were often scarce and the nights extremely uncomfortable due to the hostile elements. I pick up again paraphrasing Alan's writings:

At 3:37 p.m. the team heard the distinct sound of axes chopping in the near distance. Knowing they were coming upon the nomads, the Yuquí guides removed all their clothing in order to better identify with their jungle kin. Then, picking up their hefty bows and arrows, the naked Yuquí believers advanced forward.

Suddenly, Alan saw a brown body with a head of black hair bobbing up the trail toward them. The men immediately hid but the Yuquí woman had already spotted the missionary leading the group. Breaking off into a hysterical run, she screamed *"Abaa! Abaa!"* (the enemy).

*Yuquí woman wearing
bark rope baby sling*

The Yuquí camp broke into terrified pandemonium. Some fled while others screamed *"Abaa! Abaa!"* As the nomads fled from their camp, our men moved towards it, calling out *"Dicuateja yo che aiquio,"* (I'm the one who regards/cares about you) and other reassuring phrases. Over and over again, they called out phrases of friendship trying to reassure the nomads of the team's goodwill towards them.

At this point, the Christian Yuquí decided to take the reins and instructed the American missionaries to sit and wait for them. God's spirit emboldened Favorite Joven, one of the Christian Yuquí guides who had been so fearful in the beginning. Filled with courage he, along with Straight Hair and Wooly Hair, two of the other Yuquí guides, ran after the fleeing nomads calling out expressions of friendship and reassurance the whole while. The missionaries stayed behind pouring out their hearts to God in prayer, beseeching Him for protection and success with the contact.

The Christian Yuquí persistently extended words of camaraderie, and in time, received replies from the hostiles. *"Taso nde saa"* (Let me go to you), one of the guides called to the nomads. Fifteen minutes of reciprocal calling ensued before the wary warriors cautiously emerged from the forest's shadows and returned to their camp.

Straight Hair led a few of the nomads to the missionaries, proclaiming, "See! They are not *abaas* (enemies)!" Not long after, a fair-sized crowd of men, women, and children returned to their camp. Among them was a notably tall and muscular warrior wielding an imposing bow and bleeder-tipped arrow. His demeanor suggested a keen interest in testing his weapon on one of our men.

As the Yuquí engaged in lively exchanges in their native tongue, our men busied themselves sharpening the nomad's dull axes and machetes. A darker-skinned young woman nicknamed Giggles pointed to the missionaries' jungle boots and laughed right out loud at how ridiculous they looked, commenting, "Look! They've wrapped their feet!"

Meanwhile, the missionaries observed in silence as the Christian Yuquí animatedly conversed with their kin, all the while sharpening the nomads' machetes and axes. Encircling them stood eight robust warriors gripping formidable looking weapons. The Yuquí guides encouraged the nomads to come to our Víbora base, promising them fresh tools and repairs for their worn-out axes.

Soon the warriors expressed that they were very hungry. "The spirits of the dead are hiding the meat from us continually," they lamented. Little evidence of meat had been seen in the abandoned camps the missionaries had passed through, nor were there any meat racks. Meat was critical to the Yuquí way of life much like money is to us. Hunger had gripped them, and they bemoaned the elusive spirits who were hiding game from them. The scanty palm heart they consumed, akin to soft cabbage, provided little nourishment for the hearty carnivores.

The contact continued for over two hours. It was getting late so Alan suggested they back off and go find a place to camp for the night before it was too dark. Our men kept vigilance the whole night and lay directly on the damp ground. The next morning, they met up with the hostiles again. By 9:00 a.m., the *Bia* told our men to leave and return to the Víbora base, promising that they'd come to our camp. Knowing how hungry they were, our men were confident the nomads' promise was sincere.

Realizing they had a good chance to make it to the Víbora camp by evening, the team hightailed it for home. Alan had been sick for two days with a sore throat and high fever; no doubt, the long stressful nights lying on damp jungle ground while shivering uncontrollably had triggered the illness.

It turned out he had plenty of time to rest up once they were back at the Víbora. The warriors did not return as they promised. After waiting for two more weeks, Alan and the Yuquí guides flew back to the Chimoré base.

Having my husband back home was a joyful occasion, and he quickly settled back into the everyday routine; however, a sense of uncertainty lingered in our routines at the Chimoré. Alan's crucial role as "language bridge" meant we had to be prepared for abrupt changes, anticipating further periods of separation with all the accompanying challenges. The unpredictability of whether he would be called away to assist with new contacts, or if we would have to relocate back to the Víbora base, hindered our ability to fully engage with our duties at

Vickie with Yuquí friends

Chimoré as we once did. An entire month drifted by, shrouded in uncertainty, with no indication the nomads would reappear.

★★★★★★★

An Astounding Encounter

Roaring full speed ahead down the jungle airstrip, the airplane lifted off, then soared overhead into the wild blue yonder, leaving the children and me waving our cheerless good-byes. The elusive nomads had finally emerged at the Víbora base. Alan was on board the plane flying with two Yuquí believers. All three of them were uncertain of the duration of their stay at the Víbora.

Two-and-a-half months had passed since the fruitful meeting with the hostiles in the jungle. The starving warriors had vowed to visit the Víbora camp, lured by the promise of plentiful food, but then vanished back into the hidden recesses of the jungle, leaving the missionaries in total suspense about when or if they might show up.

The morning at the Víbora base had started with a routine inspection of the gift trail leading to the Chore River. When the missionaries arrived at the river, they were astounded by the sight on the opposite bank. A formidable band of naked brown nomads stood gripping their huge bows and arrows. The missionaries communicated to a small extent through pantomiming and offered bananas and other gifts

Grant Mayer helping with the contact

to the warriors. They managed to have a fairly smooth interaction in this manner. When the crew returned to camp, they wasted no time in alerting the Chimoré base. Hurriedly Alan and his two Yuquí companions set off to help the team at the Víbora. The Yuquí wives and families were scheduled to follow on a subsequent flight.

"Here they come!" one of the men announced. Straight Hair, Toughy, Favorite Joven, and Alan had arrived at the Víbora base the day before. By 4:00 a.m. the next morning, they made the four-kilometer trek to the Chore River where, around 9:00 a.m., the *Bia* made their appearance.

What a sight to behold—naked brown nomads cautiously trailing out of the jungle's obscure shadows onto the sandy bank of the Chore River! The missionaries had waited for so many years for this to become a reality; the hostiles coming to see us of their own volition! The thrill

The hostiles on bank of the Chore River

of the moment pulsed through Alan's veins as he gazed at the far bank. Robust warriors stood gripping their hefty bows and arrows, while others of assorted ages began clustering around them. There were more than twenty of them standing on the far bank.

The missionary crew immediately sprang into action and built a rudimentary raft from palm logs. They then secured a rope to a tree on each side of the river, allowing the raft to be pulled to and fro across the Chore by hand. This enabled them to transfer food items to the *Bia*, who were delighted with the plentiful supply of bananas and manioc. Eventually, the team communicated their intention to return to their own camp for hunting and fishing and promised to bring back meat for the jungle dwellers the next day. The prospect of receiving meat delighted the nomads.

The following day, Favorite Joven's wife, Rosa, and Toughy's wife, Justina, joined the group at the Chore River. Not being at all shy, Rosa began chatting playfully and flirtatiously across the river with her newly met kinfolk. At least two of our men stayed with the Yuquí wives on our side of the river at all times as a guard so the hostiles would think twice before causing trouble. Friendly contacts with them continued for thirteen consecutive days.

One way the team kept the nomads around was by cooking up large kettles of rice or corn. This gave them time to interact with the group. Later, Alan sat by the fire cooking a large kettle of rice sweetened with sugar, a concoction that soon became the nomad's favorite. He and those around him were momentarily distracted when the raft arrived from the other side of the river. When Alan returned, the kettle of rice was gone! Stolen!

With a voice loud enough to echo across the river, Alan stressed in the Yuquí dialect, "They took the kettle as they should not have." His tone was firm and resonant, ensuring all within earshot could grasp the gravity of his words. He then issued a clear edict, "Stop sharpening their tools! Do not bring any other gifts from the other side of the river." Directing his attention back to the hostiles, he then delivered an ultimatum: "Bring my kettle back or we will stop bringing you food."

Favorite Joven and Toughy quickly rushed to Alan's aid reiterating, "The kettle has to come back or else!" The jungle dwellers could see our men meant business! They soon started whistling to each other in characteristic Yuquí fashion; signaling and communicating with those hiding in the woods. Promptly, the kettle was retrieved and set over the fire.

This upset the matriarch of the group, who turned to Alan and ordered him to "Leave!" Recognizing this was not the time to bow to her anger, Alan responded "I need to stay and finish cooking the rice so we can show you how it is eaten." The years my husband dedicated to mastering the Yuquí language proved invaluable. Without this linguistic bridge, the incident could easily have jeopardized any potential friendship with them.

That morning witnessed a series of intense confrontations. Subsequently, one missionary ventured across the river with a generous bag of candy for the Yuquí nomads, whom we had nicknamed among ourselves for identification purposes. When the candy arrived, a formidable and unpredictable warrior we dubbed "Macho," forcefully tried to grab the bag of candy.

An unpredictable warrior

In God's providence, Alan was heading to the raft that very moment and instructed the missionary to maintain a firm grip on the bag. He called for Toughy, a Christian Yuquí comrade from the Chimoré renowned for his strength and past fervor. Toughy had previously been dubbed with that nickname for good reason! Being strong and muscular, he was remembered for choking the early missionaries when the Chimoré base was just getting established before he came to know Christ. Alan's instruction to Toughy was clear. "Take the candy and give it out to *all* the people."

Toughy took the bag and distributed the candy to *all* of the *Bia*. After receiving a fistful of the sweet delights, Macho then, much like a spoiled child, sat on a nearby log grinning from ear to ear; popping one candy after another into his mouth. It didn't take much to make Macho happy, and it didn't take much to make him mad; but when he became sullen, watch out! In a separate incident, Macho was spotted sulking and hiding in the jungle's dark shadows with a fully strung bow. Straight Hair, another Yuquí co-worker from the Chimoré, adeptly handled that situation and skillfully diffused the tension by giving Macho some added attention.

Though our men wanted to show respect to the nomads, they certainly didn't want them to be dictating all the shots. The *Bia* were still resistant to having non-Yuquí missionaries among them, so the team worked hard on getting them to accept the foreign missionaries like they did their Chimoré kinfolk.

In spite of a number of tense interactions, contact with them over the next couple of days proved successful. On the third day, the team told the *Bia* that they would be gone for two days in order to hunt and bring back meat for them. This always set well with the meat hungry warriors.

God blessed the men's hunting and fishing endeavors. When they headed back out to the Chore River two days later, their packs were loaded with meat: two large tiger-striped catfish, a red-footed tortoise, two monkeys and a tree anteater to be specific. Added to the bananas, manioc, sugar and other gifts the men displayed; the hostiles were beginning to see it was very worthwhile for them to have friendship with us.

★★★★★★★

Macho Steals the Show

A few days later the team returned to the Chore, chainsaw in hand, intending to build a makeshift bridge across the river. When they arrived, they found the nomads were already fashioning a simple bridge from saplings. Spotting an ideal tree by the water's edge, one of the missionaries skillfully sawed it down and sent the tree crashing across the river. The nomads eagerly reinforced the bridge with additional saplings. Meanwhile, Favorite Joven was busy cooking up a kettle of sweetened rice, hoping to lure the *Bia* to our side of the river and eventually to our base camp. I'll continue paraphrasing my husband's writings:

Once the bridge was finished, the wary nomads, armed with bows and arrows, cautiously traversed the log. Their unease was palpable, for they had never learned to swim. After they safely crossed to the missionaries' side of the river, they were escorted to a hut containing many gifts we planned to give them. Giggles, a young slave girl, surreptitiously took a machete and dropped it through a hole in the wall to grab later. A missionary recovered the blade while reminding his coworkers to remain extra vigilant. Any theft could jeopardize the fragile trust we were building with them. The theft wasn't merely a loss of property; it could quickly escalate into a permanent loss of our budding friendship with the nomads.

The jungle guests gathered around the fire with the missionaries, enjoying the warm sweetened rice when out of the blue, one of them announced "We want to go to your camp." What a surprise that was! "Well, let's go!" one of the missionaries' responded. By 10:00 a.m. the whole group headed for the Víbora base. What a shock the wives and children waiting back at the camp would have when their men showed up with armed naked warriors!

En route, the rainforest came alive with the sounds of a band of monkeys, prompting Toughy and Alan to step off the trail and see if they could shoot a few. Alan's .22 rifle was not well sighted in, and he had been frustrated with missing almost everything he shot at. Nevertheless, he took aim and started shooting. God intervened and directed every one of the bullets blasting from his misaligned firearm. After just four shots, he had put down five monkeys in all, one being a young one the *Bia* might keep as a pet. The hostiles were suitably impressed! The chief, known as Matador, received the prime share of the hunt, solidifying relationships between the two groups.

The nomads waited at the edge of the missionary clearing once they reached the Víbora camp while the team collected bananas to load into their palm leaf backpacks. After being fully loaded down, they turned to leave; but not before announcing, "We won't be waiting for you to cook rice for us (at the Chore River) tomorrow. Instead, we will return here to your camp. We will be bringing *yiti* (wives and children) with us to eat the rice you cook." This gesture of trust and friendship signaled a whole new chapter in our relationship with them. Clearly, progress was being made!

The next day the missionaries kept a keen eye on the gift rack, knowing the *Bia's* dark-skinned bodies seamlessly blended into the jungle's shadowy embrace. By the second day, Alan noticed some movement out by the rack in the late afternoon. Sure enough, it was them! Instead of sneaking up warily to remove the gifts, they hooted loudly instead; announcing their presence from the clearing's edge. In response, Straight Hair hooted back signaling our team was on its way.

Carrying bananas and a pot of sweetened rice, our men advanced towards the edge of the jungle. True to their word, the nomads arrived with their families, introducing new faces to the team. An easily startled teen-aged girl earned the nickname "Spooky," while two other young women were dubbed "Jane and Sunday." A pair of high-class young warriors joined the group and quickly became known as "Tom and Dick."

As the day progressed, the two Yuquí groups engaged in warm conversation by the fire. The nomadic group's discussion of ancestry with their Chimoré relatives brought a whole new revelation to them—they were not the only inhabitants on earth after all! The term *Bia,* (the people) reflected their belief in their unique existence. Everyone else was considered to be *abaa*, malevolent reincarnated spirits of their deceased who were determined to do them harm. As the hostiles pieced together relationships with their Chimoré kin, they hugged themselves ecstatically, elated to discover they weren't all alone in the vast jungle after all!

A number of missionary families living at the Víbora gradually joined the group out by the rack, carefully timing their arrival to ensure their jungle friends didn't feel threatened. As they encircled the fire, waiting for the rice to cook, the atmosphere was warm and inviting. Amidst the growing assembly, Macho decided it was his moment to shine and launched into a vivid and animated hunting tale. Only a film could have adequately captured Macho's story telling techniques, but let's just say he stole the show! Even those that didn't speak Yuquí were captivated with his performance.

Flexing his broad muscular arms, he mimicked stringing an arrow to his hefty bow; then feigned shooting at his prey (brown monkeys with gray tails). Flawlessly, he intoned the forceful loud thuds of his arrows impacting the primates and their shrieks of pain as they fled through the jungle trees. His warrior companions sitting on their haunches in typical Yuquí fashion listened with rapt attention. As the warrior parroted the loud thuds of his arrows and the agonized shrieks of pain from the monkeys, his comrades squealed with delight and hugged themselves tightly, rubbing their arms with eager anticipation. Macho's masterful display of the tantalizing hunt was Yuquí entertainment at its best!

As evening approached and rain began to fall, it did little to dampen the spirits of the Víbora team. The missionary group was elated with the successful contact, their joy undiminished by the weather. After the *Bia* left, the missionaries and their Yuquí allies immediately set out to hunt and fish. For the jungle warriors, meat was indispensable. Without meat, they considered themselves unfed. Our Yuquí coworkers and their spouses prepared the day's catch, roasting and smoking it over their campfires to have ready for the nomads the next day.

A Sour Ending

The thunderous roar of the small Cessna zooming overhead sent some of our nomadic friends fleeing for refuge in the jungle. The pilot, having just delivered supplies to the Víbora Base, chose to skim the treetops near where the nomads were congregated as he departed. Terrified, several of them fled for the jungle while others like Macho and Matador, lay calmly on the ground taking it all in. Alan had explained to the *Bia* that the loud noise of the *yatsitata* (firefly, star, airplane) during the deliveries was normal and not to worry, but he never expected the pilot to fly right overhead during a contact!

Taking advantage of the situation, the team restated to the nomads that the *yatsitata* was enroute to our faraway farm (Chimoré base) to bring them more food and some new Yuquí relatives for them to meet. By swapping Yuquí families from the Chimoré, none of them grew too exhausted with the nomad's constant demands at the Víbora. The missionaries expressed to the *Bia* that the Chimoré Yuquí group outnumbered them, hoping the jungle dwellers would eventually decide to live at the Chimoré base with their kin. This would significantly increase their chance of survival as a cultural entity as well as enlarge their gene pool.

Once the commotion subsided, the nomads gathered around the fire to wait for the kettles of rice and corn to finish cooking. My husband never ceased to be amazed as he watched some of them dip their bare hands into the boiling water to test if the corn and rice were done. It seemed traveling naked through the inhospitable jungle had toughened and desensitized their skin.

Friendly contacts continued day after day until the missionaries thought it was time to introduce the concept of trading with them.

It was crucial for the *Bia* to recognize the value of many items delivered by aircraft. Our Yuquí comrade from the Chimoré, Straight Hair, tirelessly explained the trading concept to the nomads. At last, Macho declared he wanted an ax.

Alan again clarified to the warrior that he would need to give our men two of his arrows in exchange for one ax. Macho didn't like that idea; nevertheless, he said, "Bring me an ax."

An ax was brought to him while Straight Hair clarified yet again that he would have to give up two of his arrows in exchange for one valuable ax. Matador, the chief, was quick to trade two of his arrows for an ax.

Straight Hair, right, with nomadic kin; Macho on left

Macho, on the other hand, was only interested in exchanging one of his arrows for the ax. When his offer of one arrow was rejected, the robust warrior turned around and sulked like a spoiled child. Subsequently, Wallace Pouncy went to retrieve several hatchets. Returning with them, Macho was informed that he could swap one arrow for a hatchet, but an ax would require two arrows due to its greater value. Another warrior was quick to trade his arrow for a hatchet; nevertheless, the hostiles were beginning to get edgy.

The chief's younger brother, Dick, was one of the last ones to trade an arrow for a hatchet. But as they prepared to leave, Dick turned around and demanded, "Give me my arrow back."

"Give my hatchet back, and I'll give you your arrow," Alan replied.

Dick's dissatisfaction with my husband's response escalated, prompting a more forceful stance on his part. In a bold move,

Macho intruded, and tried to grab the arrow from Alan's grasp. "I'm going to hold onto it tightly, and you'll break the arrow if you try to take it from me," Alan cautioned, summoning Straight Hair for backup. He also appealed to Matador, the chief, to restrain Macho, which he did. Yet, Macho's determination saw him continue to pry the arrow from Alan's grip.

As the event unfolded, the nomadic women began to wander away, joining others along the trail that snaked back into the rainforest. Throughout the ordeal, the chief remained composed, while Smiley remained detached and ignored the entire scene.

The retreat of the nomads signaled our men to do the same. Alan removed the kettle from the flames and began making his way back to camp. Wallace Pouncy, our colleague, lingered last in the clearing. Casting a backward glance as he departed, he spotted the notorious Macho, bow at the ready, aiming a large arrow at Alan's back from behind a jungle tree. Wallace's vehement "NO! NO! NO!" echoed, prompting the enraged warrior to slowly lower his bow before vanishing into the jungle's depths.

Contact had ended on a sour note that day. Nevertheless, the men felt some ground had been gained. The nomadic *Bia* were learning the missionaries would stand their ground and not let the warriors walk all over them with impunity. The team felt confident the nomads would be back, though they couldn't predict when.

My Return to the Víbora

As I gazed down at the lush green airstrip, I was struck by the incredible transformation since my first helicopter landing at the Víbora camp. What had once been a basic settlement of a few crude jungle houses on bare earth had blossomed into something remarkable. The missionaries had done an extraordinary job of turning the dense jungle across the river into a well-manicured airstrip and the camp had been transformed into a fully functional base. The aircraft landed with a resounding thud, and the children and I quickly disembarked. Moments later, we were wrapped in Alan's warm embrace, overjoyed to be reunited as a family.

Earlier that day, Paul and Sharon Short had taken our place at the Chimoré base, allowing us to move into their house at the Víbora. A quick shuttle by boat brought us across the river to a row of sturdy jungle houses surrounded by lush greenery. Fruit trees, nurtured over several years, were now bearing their bounty.

It didn't take long to get settled into Short's cozy two-bedroom jungle house. With raised palm wood floors, we could rest easily when the Víbora River overflowed its banks during the rainy season. The Parker family had left the camp for Spanish language study in Cochabamba.

Home Sweet Home at the Víbora River

This left the missionary team reduced to just four families: Curt and Dawn Young, Wallace and Barbara Pouncy, Grant and Alana Mayer, and us, the Fosters. Nevertheless, the base thrived with the laughter of fifteen children among us, ensuring a vibrant and playful environment for our progeny.

At that point, our Yuquí comrades from the Chimoré base had already returned to their homes. This meant we would need to have missionaries flown in to fortify our team when the nomads returned. With the sour ending of the last contact, the missionaries were left pondering as to when that might be.

We enjoyed three peaceful weeks, reuniting and settling in as a family, only to be disrupted by disturbing news over the radio: a logger had been fatally wounded by a Yuquí warrior not far from our base at the Víbora, inadvertently increasing the likelihood of military intervention.

Two weeks later, Alan's vision began to deteriorate in one eye, prompting an urgent trip to Santa Cruz for medical consultation. The diagnosis was toxoplasmosis, an infection caused by a parasitic invasion of his eye, leading to an extended stay in the city for treatment. In our absence, a Christian Yuquí couple from Chimoré took over our responsibilities at the Víbora base. Lorenzo and Antonia, who spoke rudimentary Spanish, were prepared to liaise with the missionaries and communicate with the nomads should they reemerge.

The hostiles made an unexpected appearance during our time away. Grant Mayer, Curt Young, and Lorenzo, our Yuquí comrade,

Alan and Roger inspecting Lorenzo's wound

headed out to greet them. As they drew close, Grant noticed a warrior with a fully drawn bow standing obscured among the dark shadows. "Run! They're going to shoot!" Grant yelled. Upon fleeing, a barbed arrow impacted Lorenzo in the middle of his back with such force, it threw him to the ground. The arrow, shot by the notorious warrior Macho, impacted our Yuquí comrade dangerously close to his spine. Upon hearing the grim news by radio, Alan accompanied the pilot as they evacuated Lorenzo to Santa Cruz for medical attention.

Surgery was performed and we were grateful to hear the wound wasn't as severe as first feared. Lorenzo returned to his home at the Chimoré just a few days later to recuperate among his own people. Instead of improving though, he grew feverish and much sicker, so he was flown to Cochabamba for more advanced medical care.

We joined him in Cochabamba as Alan's eye condition still needed attention. Alan oversaw Lorenzo's care and interacted with the doctor on his behalf as Lorenzo's Spanish was limited. His condition continued to deteriorate, despite X-rays showing nothing unusual. Soon, our Yuquí comrade's condition became critical, prompting an exploratory surgery that uncovered and removed a fragment of the arrow. This procedure marked a turning point, after which Lorenzo made a swift recovery.

Within two weeks, he returned home in good spirits, harboring little or no ill will toward his jungle relatives. His only wish was for his nomadic kin to experience friendship and learn of Christ's love like he had. Son of a formerly fierce and hostile Yuquí warrior himself, Lorenzo had experienced a profound transformation once he embraced the message of divine love and the sacrifice of Jesus for his transgressions. After he placed his faith in Jesus Christ as his own Savior, his heart was changed for all eternity.

> *I will give you a new heart and put a new*
> *spirit within you; I will remove from you your*
> *heart of stone... Ezekiel 36:26 NIV*

Ten weeks after Lorenzo was shot, the nomads silently returned and took gifts from the rack on the edge of our clearing without letting us know of their presence. Our men began going out at night when it was safer to replace gifts on the gift racks, and within two weeks, friendship had once again been established with the nomads. As in the past, they began sitting with us at the edge of our clearing, cooking and eating sweet rice together.

Macho was sitting with Grant Mayer while were eating and asked if he could have a chicken. Grant's chicken coop was behind his house deeper into our camp. Grant replied, "Come on, let's go get it. Let's go to my chicken pen."

Wooly Hair and Macho

Macho was hesitant to venture into our camp, but when he realized he needed to follow Grant if he wanted a chicken, he took the risk. Seeing Macho venture forth, most of the nomads jumped up and followed him. When they reached the chicken enclosure, Potbelly jumped over the chicken wire fence, snagging it, and almost tore it down. Before the others followed suit, Grant showed them the gate. The thought of getting a chicken excited another group of six, who asked to see our chickens. Alan gifted a plump old black hen to Slim. Smiley wanted one too, so Alan handed him a skinny brown laying hen he had brought over from the Chimoré base.

When the brave bunch rejoined the group who had remained at the cooking site, they remarked," We are going to keep the chickens and raise them." It was only a day or two later that the chickens were in the soup pot.

As they lost their fear coming into our camp, I had to get use to them checking out our jungle dwelling. They enjoyed lounging in our hammock, which we used as an easy chair.

Smiley had taken a shine to me and wanted to visit the house with Slim tagging along. Knowing their fondness for red material, I handed Smiley my red smock as a gift for his wife. You can imagine my surprise when the burly warrior strolled into our camp the next day, proudly wearing my red floral smock and grinning from ear to ear.

Alan showed several of the warriors around camp. When they passed the outhouses behind each missionary house, he explained what they were for. The nomads laughed heartily, thinking that was hilarious and totally ridiculous! Why on earth would anyone build a little house for *that* kind of business!

Now that the *Bia* were comfortable coming into our camp, some of them decided to accompany the missionaries across the river in a boat one day. Not only did they want to see the "firefly trail" (airstrip), but especially the bananas growing near the airstrip. While the men were gone, Tapir, Smiley's wife, started wailing, thinking she might not see her husband again. Several of the Yuquí women calmed her fears and reassured her.

Once again, we were grateful for our Yuquí coworkers who could effectively communicate with their jungle kin. How different from the initial years of contact at the Chimoré Base when the missionaries had no knowledge of the language or culture.

Another day, Alan took some of the men to check out a few other things in camp and left me sitting with some of the wives in front of our house. I grappled with ideas of how I could keep things interesting as we waited for the men to return. Remembering we had a full-length

Yuquí with Alan inspecting our camp

mirror inside, I dashed in and brought it outside.

I held the mirror in front of myself with my back to them, then stepped a little to one side to show them how it reflected a perfect image of me. Several stood up to touch the glass wonderingly. One of them, a heavy-set woman (having been well-nourished by her high-class husband), stepped in front of the mirror. She stood spellbound for a moment, gaping at her reflection. Then, with a smile of deep satisfaction, she stroked her hair as though preening herself, totally enthralled with her image. I didn't think she was one of the more attractive women, but she thought otherwise. Vanity runs deep in the best of us. The other women followed suit. Even some of the warriors enjoyed admiring themselves in front of the reflective glass.

It was only two days later that our men went hunting for the first time with a small group of the nomads. Straight Hair and Alan took three of the nomads with them: Smiley, Potbelly, and Dick. Alan and Straight Hair carried .22 rifles and the nomads carried their bows and arrows. Potbelly was Dick's slave and was along to carry the game home and retrieve any arrows that might lodge in a tree or swamp. They were only gone for two hours and came back to camp with fifty pounds of game. Not bad for a first hunt together!

Trading was going better with the nomads, now that they understood the more valuable items required something in return. Their worldview did not include cities nor money, so the missionaries kept things simple. In their minds, their small group and the other bands of Yuquí from which they had split were the center of the universe. Outsiders were thought to be reincarnated spirits of their dead intent on doing them harm, so it was safer to shoot them.

They believed the airplane came from the place in the sky where the spirits of their dead lived and assumed we were able to communicate, in some way, with those spirits and with Big Father (God), the new and most powerful Spirit we were beginning to introduce to them. For the most part, they seemed to believe that we foreigners were their reincarnated ancestors.

On this particular day, we traded quite a few items. Matador and Grandma each wanted a kettle. Slim, Harry, and Macho each brought an arrow to trade for kettles. There were no complaints that afternoon when they parted ways with their arrows to receive shiny new aluminum cooking pots in return.

They began talking about a lady back in their camp who was currently in labor and having a difficult time giving birth. We were able to ascertain that the woman was Giggles, slave to *Tä*, the tribal matriarch. Almost daily, they brought reports that *Tä* had not improved but continued very ill. If only *Tä* was nearby we could help her medically, but their camp was several kilometers away, and they rejected our requests to be taken to help her.

A very sick Tä in the hammock

Hunting together soon became a daily event. They had lost all fear of boats, so the guys could haul them up or downriver to hunt in areas of jungle less frequented. None of the nomadic warriors wanted to be left out of the exciting hunting trips, and one day, as the fellas headed downriver in the boat, they heard loud hollering from behind. Turning around, they saw Macho sprinting along the riverbank with his bow and arrows, frantic to join the hunting party.

Giggles was successful at giving birth, but the nomads let us know they weren't feeding her. They made it clear they didn't want to waste food on the female slave since her mistress, *Tä*, appeared close to death. Once again, both the Yuquí from the Chimoré and Alan explained to them that Big Father did not want them to kill anyone to accompany someone who died. Sadly, the custom was so ingrained they just ignored our admonitions. Fear of the dead person's spirit was a powerful motivator, and they were convinced that if they didn't send someone along to serve *Tä* in death, her spirit would get revenge and punish them. In their thinking, they had to appease her spirit. Their well-being depended on it.

Alan continued sharing biblical truths with small groups of the *Bia* each day. Slim listened intently and gave occasional feedback through comments and questions.

A larger group of the nomads showed up one day. Matador, the chief announced, "We are going to travel to a faraway place. *Tä* (mother) is very sick, and we don't want her to die here, or this place will become a place of sadness for us, and we won't want to come back. It's better if she dies far away."

Straight Hair responded, "Big Father does not want you to kill anyone else if your mother dies. He will protect you from her spirit, so don't kill anyone else." That exhortation did not sit well with Matador who mumbled under his breath.

Knowing that on their travels, they were likely to steal from Bolivian farms, Alan spoke up. "If you need bananas or manioc while you are gone, send someone to our camp to get them from us. Don't take them from the enemy (Bolivian) farms, or they will shoot you." While the chief verbally agreed to send someone for bananas, we knew it was unlikely he would follow through. He and the other warriors in the clan were arrogantly confident in their ability to avoid being shot by the farmers.

During the following eight days leading up to their departure, we reminded them not to kill anyone or steal from the farmers, although we knew the odds were low that they would heed our admonitions. Our team began praying fervently that God would remove the obstacles that were hindering the *Bia* from hearing about His redemptive plan for them.

By now, the missionary team was very weary from the continual challenges and pressures of interacting daily with the nomads, whom we knew could quickly turn unreasonably violent. Our Yuquí co-workers flew back to the Chimoré base, and another Yuquí family was flown in to replace them. The nomads paid their last visit to the Víbora River Base before leaving on their extended trip. It was anybody's guess how long they might be gone.

Alan and I flew to Cochabamba to take three weeks of much needed rest. Though we looked forward to a break, our hearts were heavy. Everyone knew the Yuquí were leaving to find a place for *Tä* to die. With her death, Giggles, her slave, as well as her newborn infant, would doubtless be killed to accompany *Tä's* spirit and enter a Christless eternity.

Piglets and Buzzers

Alan had more than one objective in mind when he visited the farm at our mission boarding school. He saw the hefty black and white Hampshire pigs as potential drawing cards to lure the nomads into our Víbora camp, not to mention their floppy-eared cousins, the Poland Chinas.

Not long after, a flight arrived at our Víbora base bearing four plump weaner piglets, two male and two female, which elicited an enthusiastic response from me: "GOOD GRIEF! What in the world are we going to do with FOUR pigs!"

Undeterred by my apparent distaste for his porcine fortunes, Alan went right to work fencing in a portion of the jungle next to camp so his fat little piglets could frolic and forage. As he headed back to camp that day, he realized our co-worker, Curt Young, was frantically signaling for him to hurry over to the houses.

The stalk of bananas on the gift rack had disappeared, snatched by the elusive nomads who then vanished into the jungle's dark shadows. The silent gift rack stood as a reminder of the lack of communication with them since the unfortunate incident with Lorenzo. Approaching the edge of the jungle with his co-workers, Alan called out in the Yuquí dialect. No response. It had been four and a half months since Lorenzo had been shot in the back.

The men hung a jug of rice, some hard candy, and thread 30 minutes beyond the clearing where the *Bia* had previously taken gifts. They discovered footprints there as well as an area where palm leaf packs had been made to carry away the bananas.

For days, our missionary team maintained a vigilant watch over the gift rack beyond the clearing, hoping to spot the elusive *Bia* before they retreated back into the rainforest. The gifts remained untouched for six days.

It was a Sunday morning and the entire missionary team had gathered at our house to worship God and study the Scriptures. Alan moved over to sit next to me and asked, "Can you see the gifts on the rack?"

"Almost."

"Almost" wasn't good enough, so he stood up and peered out towards the rack. The gifts were gone! Immediately, the guys hightailed it out to the rack where Alan called out to the warriors. No response. That afternoon, a further discovery was made: all the gifts laid out towards the Chore River had also been taken.

By the following morning, Alan was back at work on his pig enclosure while a coworker in camp was designated to watch the gift rack. At 11:00 a.m., three nomads tentatively emerged from the jungle's obscure shadows. Most of the nomads hid in the jungle while sending their ever-expendable slaves, Giggles, Potbelly, and Friday, out initially to see what kind of welcome they'd receive.

With bananas in hand, Alan and his co-workers headed back to the rack carrying more fruit. He called out to the warriors, most of whom peered cautiously from farther back in the rainforest. Soon, Matador (the chief) emerged from the jungle. "We aren't angry with you," Alan assured the chief in their dialect. "We won't shoot you." Then he approached closer to the gift rack, set the bananas down, and backed away. "Come get the bananas."

The warriors in the woods were still reluctant to show themselves. Alan removed his shirt and laid it on the ground along with his gun to show them we had no intent on revenge. Emboldened by his gesture, Giggles and Potbelly approached him. Soon ten naked nomads emerged from the shadows to join the slaves, making thirteen in all.

The team loaded up the *Bia* with bananas and manioc. "I'll tell the *yatsitata* (airplane) to bring "your others" (their Chimoré kin) to see you," Alan declared. Without further ado, the *Bia* picked up their loads and retreated into the jungle. That afternoon, Wooly Hair, Straight Hair, Lorenzo, and Toughy were all flown from the Chimoré base to reinforce our Víbora missionary team.

For the next several days, my husband seemed to be in a profound state of rumination. Watching his pensive demeanor, I deduced that he was concocting some new scheme in the shadowy corners of his mind. Indeed, he was! He had devised a fresh tactic: "If we can't see them taking the gifts, then I'll make sure we *hear* them!"

Come morning, he was outside, tinkering with a new contraption. With his new invention in tow, he strode towards the gift stand. From my vantage point at the kitchen sink, I watched and wondered as I scrubbed dirty dishes. I observed him digging a shallow furrow stretching from the gift rack to our house. Finished with that, he hauled out a long lamp cord (over one hundred yards worth!) and laid it in the trench, then covered it all with dirt. "What could he possibly be plotting now?" I wondered.

When he returned, he revealed his clever stratagem to me. He had attached a spring-activated plank to the gift rack's cross bar. It dangled under the weight of the bananas, but once the weight was removed, the spring propelled the plank upwards, causing two metal pieces to come in contact. This completed a circuit which triggered a battery-operated buzzer near our kitchen sink. We had a good view of the gift rack from there. I was given *strict* instructions to turn the buzzer off before dashing out to alert him, so the circuit wouldn't blow.

"I'm heading out to the rack," He informed me. "Stay here while I go remove the stalk of bananas. If the buzzer sounds, make sure you turn the switch *off,* so it doesn't blow a circuit."

He ventured toward the edge of the jungle. Sure enough, upon removing the bananas, a resounding "BUZZZZZZZ" filled the air near my window. I hastily turned the alarm off.

A few days later, Alan was perched in his outdoor office, the mission radio hour prattling away, when a peculiar buzzing interrupted the broadcast. Baffled momentarily, he soon realized it was the alarm inside our house causing all the racket. As he bounded down the steps from his office to turn the switch off, I was already dashing out the front door to notify him the alarm had sounded. Practically colliding in our haste, he snapped, "Turn the switch off!" after which he promptly rushed off to greet the nomads.

I dashed back inside, only to be instantly spellbound by the scenario outside our kitchen window (as the buzzer buzzed...and buzzed). Just beyond the clearing, the jungle's emerald embrace framed a pair of bronze-colored nomads illuminated by the sun's golden rays. They were removing a large stalk of bananas from the rack. What a sight to behold, one that still lingers in my memory to this day! The incessant *buzzing* abruptly jerked me out of my reverie. I rushed to turn the switch off, grateful it hadn't caused an electrical mishap—a secret Alan would discover only upon reading my memoir.

In the meantime, Alan and Lorenzo approached the rack, hooting in typical Yuquí fashion to let the nomads know they were coming. Warily, the chief emerged from out of the jungle depths with Smiley and Slim following close behind. By then, our Yuquí comrade, Straight Hair, had joined Alan and Lorenzo. They insisted Matador, Slim, and Smiley leave their bows and arrows behind before approaching them.

A dialogue with the warriors unfolded, shedding light on the reasons for the recent event in which a colonist was shot through with their treacherous arrows. Our men learned that Macho's child had been kidnapped at the Chore River, prompting him to retaliate against a Bolivian woodsman with a barrage of arrows. Meanwhile, the mission airplane, already bound to our Víbora base to transport our Yuquí coworkers back home, returned to the Chimoré base. Our Yuquí comrade's families were then flown over to join them for interacting with the hostiles.

The following day, late in the afternoon, we had pretty much given up on the nomads returning. Quite a bit of hubbub was going on in camp at the time: motors running, chickens clucking, wives chatting as the children played and hollered outdoors. Suddenly, a loud and unexpected *"BUZZZZZZZZ"* resounded from our house. Alan rushed to our place to deactivate the switch and looked out the window to see a fair-sized group of cinnamon-colored nomads clustered around the gift rack. How grateful he was for his secret weapon, or the nomads would have left without any meaningful exchange with us. He rushed out and was approaching the gift rack when one curious warrior called out to him, "How did you know we were here?"

Feeling a tad dishonest, my husband responded, "I heard you." This left the furtive *Bia* taken aback. Unbeknownst to the warriors, Alan had a clandestine ace up his sleeve: the buzzer! Being late afternoon, the encounter was brief before they vanished back into the wilderness, yet they vowed to come back the following day.

Alan's ingenious buzzer mechanism led to thirty-five consecutive contacts with the hostiles from that day onward. We engaged almost daily with the nomads for almost five weeks, experiencing both friendly and nerve-racking exchanges that stirred mixed emotions within us. The insight of our Yuquí allies from the Chimoré base was indispensable in discerning the fluctuating temperaments of the hostiles.

To manage the continual contacts, we arranged regular supply flights to bring alternate Yuquí families from the Chimoré. This gave our Yuquí advisors at the Víbora a respite from the constant demands of their jungle kin. Those of us living at the Víbora base, however, were under extreme stress, especially our men. After long and grueling days appeasing the hostiles, the guys had to take off on evening hunting and fishing excursions to satisfy the protein cravings of the hungry warriors and their families.

During the team's initial meeting with the nomads, the chief, Matador was delighted to receive a capybara and a sizable electric eel. The *Bia* consumed almost any animal except snakes. Two alligators were also gifted to him that day, a rare delicacy for the jungle dwellers.

Unlike before, our men insisted they all sit a short distance into our clearing rather than close to the gift rack at the edge of the jungle. This precaution was taken even though it meant our men were still within range of potential arrow shots from

Matador, Chief of the Víbora group

the shelter of the jungle. Despite this, our men's stance was clear: they distrusted the warriors. The nomads would need to make a real effort to regain our trust.

★★★★★★★

An Intimate Escapade

Ahh... the sweet bliss of having some time alone, just the two of us. This joy was ours to relish, thanks to our missionary friend, Roger Nebergall, who was resolute in ensuring we had one evening exclusively for ourselves. The preceding weeks had been a whirlwind of demands and stress for both Alan and me, marked by the relentless daily interchanges with the unpredictable hostiles at the Víbora base. In the midst of all the hustle and bustle, our friend flew to the Víbora to lend our team a hand.

Roger graciously offered to spend the night with our children, hoping to give Alan and me the luxury of some much-needed time together, just the two of us. I was delighted! After doing some mental gymnastics, Alan consented. Eager to enjoy a nice restaurant or pass the night in a hotel down river, I packed my bags. Not! Neither restaurants nor hotels could be found on our remote jungle river, so we did the next best thing. Assisted

The Víbora River and camp in dry season

by my personal Indiana Jones, Alan loaded the canoe with our pup tent, sleeping bags, paddles, and a .22 rifle. After kisses and hugs for the kiddos, we were off on our "intimate" escapade.

"Would you like to try paddling in back?" My hubby asked before getting into the canoe. The river was low and didn't look too intimidating. "Sure!" I responded enthusiastically.

Knowing it was the perfect hour for wild game to come to the riverbank, Alan happily sat in front with a loaded rifle. I could see we were in for a real "romantic" getaway.

A cacophony of sounds pulsated through the humid jungle air as evening fell: cicadas thrummed, frogs croaked, birds performed their twilight choruses while the ever-annoying mosquitoes buzzed our ears. I stroked the brown, tannin-stained waters while Alan quietly sat at the front studying the dark river's waters and bank.

My skills with a paddle were laughable at best; nevertheless, I paddled with steely determination, striving to be as quiet as possible, only making the occasional clunk or splash at the stern. Alan, ever the silent stalker at the prow, was ready to fire at a moment's notice, eyeing the bank for a thirsty peccary or tapir. Not long into our journey, my sporadic splashes got the best of him. He glanced back, whispering, "Is there a chance you could paddle a tad quieter?" "Doing my best," I muttered, pushing us onward and grimacing whenever my stroke clunked the side of the canoe. Attempting to navigate the craft in stealth proved a lot trickier than I anticipated.

Like a good sport, the hunter up front tolerated the sporadic plunks, flumps, and plonks from the rear, but when the canoe kept veering toward the bank, he knew the gal in back didn't have a clue what she was doing. Realizing his guidance was needed, he turned around to instruct me on the art of silent paddling and steering. With his directives, I was able to get back on course.

Pleased to see I was handling the strokes more gently, Alan turned to resume his hushed observations at the front. Stealthily we advanced, all the while his eyes probing the murky depths and darkening banks.

Hey, I think I'm getting the hang of this, I reflected triumphantly as the paddle cut through the water without a sound. My heart swelled with jubilation, but my delight soon faded after noticing the canoe had developed a slight leftward list. Muttering Alan's instructions under my breath, I tried correcting our course, but to no avail. It didn't take long before the canoe hugged the left bank. "Just pull up and we'll trade places," Alan instructed, putting an end to his front-seat hunting aspirations.

"Ah, now this is more like it!" I exhaled in relief as I settled into the front seat. With a handsome and capable navigator at the helm, I could relax and enjoy the jungle's nocturnal chorus. This one-night get away might not be so bad after all! We continued in hushed silence as the intensifying darkness began to envelope us. Soon Alan stopped paddling to shine a flashlight over the murky water. Dozens of gleaming bright eyes peered back at us from just above the water line.

"I hope those aren't what I think they are," I murmured nervously. "Don't worry, they're just small alligators," Alan reassured, judging their size from the spacing of the eyes.

Eventually, we reached a sandy shore nice enough to set the tent up when Alan's gaze fell upon large paw prints in the sand. "Seems a jaguar stopped by for a drink," he noted.

"A jaguar? Yikes! Maybe we need to look for another beach," I suggested.

"Nah, we'll be all right. I'll have my rifle with us in the tent," he replied nonchalantly, and promptly began setting up our formidable fortress: a little ol' pup tent.

After arranging the sleeping bags, we settled inside. Alan put the gun on safety and laid it between us. "If you hear anything in the night that bothers you, just wake me up. The gun is right here. Now try to get some sleep." With that, my capable woodsman gave me a smooch on the lips, turned over, and went out like a light.

"Get away for the night and have some special time alone, just the two of you," Roger had suggested. *Yeah, just the two of us, just Alan and me... hidden in the depths of this beast-infested jungle... all alone,* I mused.

I think my hearing has never been so acute as that night while lying in that little pup tent, with Alan's snores as a soundtrack. With ears glued to that flimsy canvas wall, I listened, and I listened, and I listened, every sound amplified tenfold. Why, I think I even heard the ants come marching two by two— hurrah, hurrah.

Lying perfectly still, I listened for any telling rustling, half expecting a hungry jaguar to come sniffing at our tent door. A single clawed lunge could spell the end of our pup tent and us for that matter! I don't know at what ungodly hour I finally drifted off to sleep, but thanks to my mega eardrums, dawn greeted us unscathed.

Alan sprang out of bed as perky as a squirrel on espresso that early dawn, eager to pack up the tent and shove off in the canoe. Meanwhile, I tried to pry my eyes open with the enthusiasm of a sloth, dragging myself to the canoe's prow. We would reach camp during the morning hours, but the looming day promised a marathon of mommy duties for me. As we glided through the clear tannin-colored waters with the sun playing peek-a-boo through the canopy, and the rainforest orchestra in full swing, I solemnly vowed: *If ever again the idea of a romantic get-away in this wild beast-filled jungle is proposed, I'll decline.* Nothing says Home Sweet Home like the sight of our little jungle house after a night in the wild.

Little Turtle

My kitchen window became a porthole for capturing what soon became a regular morning occurrence. The once elusive nomads no longer hid in the jungle like before, but stood at the gift rack and alerted us of their arrival by whistling or hooting in typical Yuquí fashion.

As our interactions with them continued day after day, Alan encouraged our Christian Yuquí comrades to step up communicating with them. The most important reason we were there was to share the Good News of the Gospel! Straight Hair took this to heart and eagerly shared God's truth with his jungle kin, introducing *Papaguasu* (Big Father) as a word for God. He told them of God's love for them and the divine purpose for those he created. The *Bia* listened intently but seemed to compare this "god guy" with their "spirits along the sky".

Never before had they heard about a supreme being. Spirits in the afterlife? Oh yes. But the idea of a God who created everything? That was a concept totally foreign to them. Macho, in particular, seemed captivated by Straight Hair's words. Although understanding God's truth would be a slow process, sharing His Word with them was a priority for our missionaries. Satan had done a masterful job of blinding and clouding their minds with his lies.

> ... *He couldn't stand the truth because there wasn't a shred of truth in him. When the Liar speaks, he makes it up out of his lying nature and FILLS the world with his LIES. John 8:44 MSG*

Repeatedly, our men warned the *Bia* not to shoot at the nationals. As they listened, Straight Hair disclosed how loggers had lain in ambush for days in order to kill the nomads after their last shooting. "The *abaa* (nationals/enemies) have dogs to chase and corner you; then, they will kill you with their guns. The *abaa* set tiger traps and devise other ways to hunt you. Stop shooting them or they will go after you and kill you!"

Before leaving our camp, the nomads informed us, "We are going on a two-day *juä* (overnight trip) and then we will return to you again."

While our men appreciated them giving advance notice of their absence, they reiterated once again, "Stay far away from the *abaas* (enemies) while you are gone, and don't steal bananas from their farms. If you need bananas, come to us."

We weren't expecting any visitors the next day but at 8:30 a.m., I peered out my kitchen window to see a small group of nomads standing at the gift rack. They signaled their presence with a low drawn-out whistle that gradually ascended to a high note. Just four people made a visit that morning: Macho, Old One-Eye, Slim, and Harry. We were informed that others in the group had decided not to travel because some of them were sick. After loading up the four with bananas, one of them turned to ask my husband, "*Detibotibo mama tasää*" (Can I try some of your leftovers)?

I happened to have some leftover pumpkin pie I had made from winter squash. Alan brought the pie out to them, and the four warriors smacked their lips with pleasure and slapped the back of their heads approvingly. Another missionary brought out some brownies which were also a big hit. The warriors were invited to stay longer while our men started a kettle of rice to cook over the fire. Their visit proved to be profitable, and they promised to come back the following day.

The time came for Straight Hair and his wife to return to their home. He let the nomads know he would be flying back to his home at the big farm (the Chimoré Base). He explained to them that the farm provided much of the manioc and bananas we were gifting to them. The news that Straight Hair was leaving really troubled the chief. "Well, if you all (our Yuquí kin) return to your big farm, they (the foreign missionaries) might kill us."

"Not so! The missionaries are the ones who own the big farm. They are the ones planting the manioc and bananas for you," Straight Hair explained to Matador. "They are your friends. They will not harm you even if we (your Yuquí kin) return to our home at the big farm."

The chief turned around, looked directly at Alan, and said, "*Oo guriquio tuti na che rese*" (He has his hands on me fully), a strong Yuquí expression to say that someone has their loving hands on you and cares for you. Needless to say, Alan was thrilled beyond words! The chief was beginning to recognize our love and concern for their welfare. Now, if only the rest of the nomads would come to the same understanding.

I had acquired a special fondness for Potbelly, a slave who was very abused and undernourished. By this time, the *Bia* had grown to respect Alan and me. Being his wife, I occasionally took liberties by taking the upper hand. One day, I left the house with a large, fluffy biscuit

Potbelly

for Potbelly. When I handed the bread to him, his master, Dick, promptly grabbed it out of his slave's hand and began to eat it. "*Ti*" (no)! I responded with a stern glare and all the authority I could muster. Then looking directly into Potbelly's eyes, I commanded: "*De tu eu!*" (You eat it instead.) Potbelly happily obeyed and stuffed the biscuit into his mouth while his sheepish-looking master stood to one side. Score!

Weeks followed and our rapport with the nomadic tribe only deepened, culminating in an open demonstration of the chief's

trust in us. This was highlighted when he brought his wife, Vera, to our camp for the first time. She emerged from the dense foliage cradling their youngest, Little Turtle, in her arms. The child was too young to walk, but when he reached the age to learn, it would be with great difficulty. Both of Little Turtle's feet were rotated inwards at the ankle leaving him clubfooted. Intermarriage with close relatives was common among the small numbered bands of Yuquí and the effects were noticeable in both groups. One Yuquí

Little Turtle before surgery

from the Chimoré had two thumbs and Little Turtle was born with club feet.

A few years later, a Bolivian doctor graciously offered to correct Little Turtle's feet at no cost. By that time, the chief's widow had complete confidence in entrusting their little boy into our care. Little Turtle clung to us for comfort and security as the three of us flew to Cochabamba for the operation. What a privilege it was to be by this precious child's side during that painful transition. Thanks to the good-hearted doctor, Little Turtle grew up walking just like his siblings.

Little Turtle arriving home after surgery

A Heartbreaking Absence

The Víbora River in rainy season

The Víbora River had overflowed its banks, flooding our camp and surrounding jungle. Creatures desperate to find higher ground found refuge near our houses. One treacherous fer-de-lance, a venomous snake of the pit viper family, thought the steps leading into our house was a perfect place to wait out the flood, while a sixty-six-inch-long bushmaster (a more deadly viper) found sanctuary in a small dry area of jungle where our men were cutting palm boards. Despite heightened vigilance, the large pit viper's appearance gave them quite a scare.

Sometime later, I looked out my kitchen window to see a javelina (peccary) frantically swimming through the flood waters right behind the house. Our meat supply was seriously low, so Alan grabbed an ax, waded through the water, and gave the starving animal a merciful blow over the head. While preparing the game, he noticed how squeaky clean the animal's digestive system was, indicating it hadn't eaten for days on end. That evening, fresh pork was added to the pressure cooker. Seasoned well in a delicious

Vickie stepping out during a flood

gravy, the tenderized pork was a nice addition to our rice. God was providing meat for us even during the flood.

We were only halfway through the rainy season and water still flowed under our house. I resorted to laundering clothes on the porch and dried them behind the kerosene refrigerator where heat was emitted. Even though the water was beginning to recede, we held little hope the nomads would return.

Not many days after the flood went down, Alan was relaxing in his hammock when the tranquility of the afternoon was shattered by a high pitched buzzzzz. Leaping out of his "easy chair" hammock, he switched the alarm off before heading straight out to the gift rack while I notified our coworkers. Alan advanced with a stalk of bananas just far enough so that if the hostiles were hiding in the jungle's shadows, they could see him. Then he began calling out in their dialect. With no hesitation, ten copper-skinned naked nomads emerged from the shadowy depths. Alan proceeded forward to greet them.

Something was unusual about their appearance this time. My husband immediately noticed the conspicuous absence of their elite men, all the seasoned warriors and hunters. Two youthful high-ranking men, Tom and Dick, stood among a small group of women and slaves: Harry, Potbelly, Friday, Sunday, Jane, Grandma, Spooky, and Vera. Tom and Dick, barely past their teenage years, were the chief's younger brothers and seemed to have assumed leadership of the group.

Alan drew in closer and could see the nomads' time away from us had not gone well. Some of the *Bia* were just gaunt shadows of their former selves and Grandma, having lost forty or fifty pounds, was almost unrecognizable.

They were all ravaged by hunger. Grandma and Vera, the chief's wife, were especially emaciated and covered in gray ashes. The depth of their sorrow was palpable, with Vera, so overwhelmed with despair, she could barely speak. Matador, her husband, was nowhere in sight. Typically, the chief was the first one to approach once the slaves made sure things were safe.

Alan squatted beside the chief's wife and quietly murmured, "Where is my older brother?" at which Vera began to weep. She expressed something about "the ones along the sky" (spirits of the dead). Immediately, he suspected the chief had died. Being considered family among the Chimoré Yuquí, Alan had been required early on to use kinship terms when referring to the nomads.

By now, the other missionary men had joined my husband and brought more stalks of bananas. Alan then edged over and squatted down next to Grandma. Speaking in gentle hushed tones, he inquired, "Where are my younger brothers? Why haven't they come to see me?" Overcome with emotion, Grandma too broke down weeping and responded similarly to what Matador's wife had said, something about "the ones along the sky."

Alan and Dick

With the chief gone, his two younger siblings, Tom and Dick, seemed to be left in charge of the forlorn group. They sat with Alan, engaging in conversation with him. Meanwhile, the women began to weave palm leaf backpacks to load the bananas in. After a couple of hours, the grief-stricken wanderers retreated back into the jungle's shrouded depths, each one bidding farewell with *"Eyeguatu,"* (keep yourself warm) as they filed into the woods.

Five days after this initial contact, we received news by radio from the Chimoré base that three Bolivian loggers and three nomads had been killed along the Chore River north of us. Could it be that all the mature men in the group were killed in a deadly clash with the *abaa*, the enemy? Perhaps a few, but all of them? Was this the reason the women responded with such grief when Alan asked them about their key men? How many more would be lost before we had the opportunity to share the Good News with them? It seemed Satan's forces were prevailing, but in God's mysterious ways, He was working behind the scenes to save the rest of this floundering group from the devil's wretched hold.

Three weeks elapsed before they returned, again with the noticeable absence of all their seasoned leaders and hunters. This left only Tom and Dick to lead. We cooked sweetened rice for them at the edge of the clearing. After a couple of hours, Dick seemed eager to leave, prompting the rest of them to pack bananas into their palm-leaf sacks. Alan explained that they had brought the nomads fewer bananas this time because we wanted them to return to us sooner. They seemed to understand.

We were just finishing up lunch the following day, when Alan glanced out our kitchen window to see a shadowy form slide into view at the edge of the jungle. He headed straight out to the gift rack. Thanks to God's abundant blessings on our men's hunting and fishing endeavors the previous night, they were able to present the nomads with three alligators, eight or nine good sized fish and four young ducks. Our Yuquí friends from the Chimoré base had already begun to roast the game behind their dwelling and extended an invitation for the nomads to join them in the feast.

Initially, Tom and Dick were wary, so sent two expendable slaves along with Grandma to make sure things were safe. So much for looking after their elderly! Eventually the rest joined them, and they sat around the smoke rack. A new fire was kindled to prepare some sweetened rice. The nomads were also presented with several chickens, much to the delight of Spooky, a young girl among them. The group discussed the possibility of hunting together the next morning and it was decided to meet them at the Chore River.

Our men reached the Chore at dawn but found themselves all alone. They hooted in typical Yuquí fashion for thirty minutes before they received an answering hoot. Then, they waded through chest-deep water to join the nomads on the other side, a short distance from the river bank, but the band seemed in no hurry at all to go hunting. Before long, grief overwhelmed the nomads once again, causing them to weep uncontrollably. They wailed and intoned eerie chants to the spirits of their deceased, consumed by sorrow and despair.

In their anguish, Vera and Grandma implored Alan to kill them and end their suffering, feeling like life had lost all meaning without their men.

"No. We are the ones who care deeply for you. We will protect and feed you," Alan reassured them. Not long after, rain threatened so the hunting trip was canceled. "We'll come back to hunt tomorrow if it isn't raining and bring sugar for you."

"Come back to us," they replied. Before disappearing into the jungle, they turned to say, *"Eyeguatu,"* (keep yourselves warm by the fire).

The missionaries could see Tom and Dick were floundering without the leadership of their mature men, looking to Vera, the chief's widow, for guidance. This gave Alan hope that they might look to us for counsel and consider relocating and joining their kin at the big farm (Chimoré base). The odds of Tom and Dick providing enough food from the jungle for the entire group seemed impossible. They needed our help, but could we persuade them to accept it?

The following day, the groups met again at the Chore River. After visiting for a while, Dick said, "Let's go hunting," and off they went. They weren't having much success, so they headed back. Alan suggested "Let's circle around and return to your camp."

"Op!" (No!) Tom emphatically objected. *"Yiti* (the children) will be frightened," Vera, the chief's widow, retorted.

"You need to help your children lose their fear of us," Alan interjected.

They all continued through the jungle until they reached our gift trail on the nomad's side of the Chore River. The *Bia* must have been close to their camp because several of them stopped and hooted. Soon others emerged from the jungle to join them. The team shared lunch with the group and then left. By that time, the Chore River had risen considerably, and our men had to swim to reach the other side. From there, they hiked back to the Víbora camp.

During that four-day trip, God granted our men several excellent visits with the *Bia*. Not only did they hunt together but gathered around the fire to eat and listen to Biblical truths. Favorite Joven had flown over from the Chimoré and outdid himself in

Favorite Joven on the right

conveying divine truth, capturing the undivided attention of his highly attentive audience.

Rather than hike the four kilometers back to the Víbora base one night, the guys camped on the opposite side of the Chore River from the nomads, planning on hunting howler monkeys with them the next morning; however, the howler monkeys remained silent throughout the next day, thus sparing their lives.

By then, the water in the Chore had dropped to where the *Bia* could cross, so they accompanied our men back to our Víbora base. On the way, the nomads revealed a much shorter trail of their own to our men, showcasing their growing confidence in the missionaries. The small band was noticeably trusting us more and more. The warriors were loaded up with bananas, sugarcane, cloth, and fishlines. As they prepared to leave, they promised to return to our camp the next day. Since the Chore was still dangerously high, the team doubted they would really show up.

The following morning Alan, accompanied by four others, left the Víbora base and waited at the Chore River until midday. Repeatedly they called out and hooted, hoping for another reunion with the nomads. Hearing no response, they decided to look around and came upon an abandoned Yuquí camp. There were no nomads in sight.

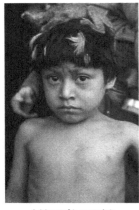

A Yuquí boy with squirrel monkey

As they continued onward, they heard someone approaching in the background. Tapir and her four young children, all under four years, were heading to their campsite. Being alone, she was overcome with terror at seeing the team until our men reassured her and calmed her down. Eventually, others showed up. Vera, the deceased chief's wife, brought out her six children: Little Squirrel and his doppelganger, a younger sister, Little Turtle (Clubfoot), and two other children. Ultimately, twenty-four nomads showed up, the only survivors of their recent tragedy!

Knowing that a third of the band had perished during their previous four-month trip, our men felt heartbroken. Favorite Joven devoted much of the time offering comfort and spiritual guidance. Shortly after noon, the team left and let the nomads know that they were going to make a bridge across the Chore River so the Yuquí could come to us more easily. They felled trees into the river from each bank to create a rustic bridge before heading for home.

The following day, the team lingered at the Chore until midday, hoping the *Bia* would emerge from the jungle. They chose not to search for the nomad's camp, thinking they might not be welcomed. After calling into the jungle several times, they turned to make the trek back home. On the way, they hunted monkeys and turkeys to provide meat for our Yuquí coworkers to roast over their fires. Once again, we faced a long, four-month wait, wondering how many of our jungle friends would survive until their next return.

Potbelly's Risky Endeavors

It was the middle of the year, and time again for our yearly mission conference at the boarding school. While we were there, missionaries from Santa Cruz shared news they had seen on television: a settler had been fatally attacked by the Yuquí hostiles in the Chore River region. It was a somber realization that the *Bia* were busy retaliating for the loss of their own during their time away from us.

After a week of uplifting sessions and camaraderie with fellow missionaries, we returned to the Víbora Base with renewed vigor. Alan was honing his language skills in his study, when he decided to take a break and make some tea. As he waited for the water to boil,

Alan studying the language

he casually glanced out the window. An obscure figure flitted by behind the gift rack.

"I think I just saw one of the *Bia*," he informed me. I rushed to alert our coworkers while Alan left for the jungle's edge hooting to the nomads the whole while. By the time the other men arrived, the nomads had already come out without hesitation. They followed our men to gather bananas. Our team was extremely generous, thinking it would be better to have the *Bia* go away happy than not return.

Alan mentioned to them that we had received news that some of the *abaas* (enemies) had been shot. His comment immediately grabbed their attention. "Did they die? What kind of feathers were on the arrows?" they inquired, obviously wanting to identify which of their arrows had accomplished their murderous intentions.

During their time away, our sows had welcomed some new piglets, so Alan generously offered one each to Tom, Dick, and Tapir. They nestled the squealing piglets in flour sacks to carry them back to their camp yet allowed them to roam freely near the fire where everyone enjoyed eating sweetened rice.

The *Bia* didn't hesitate to enter our camp the next day, heading straight for the house where our Yuquí colleagues resided. Hunting had been good the night before, so the smoke rack was heaped with meat. I invited some of the women to follow me to a hut where we stored used clothing and gave items to each of them. The women were very pleased with the sugar cane I included as well as the clothing.

Steve Parker and Grant Mayer with the nomads

Most of the group had come to see us that day, leaving behind their youngest children supervised by two older boys back at their camp. As they gathered around the fire, Alan took the opportunity to share more about the eternal nature of *Papaguasu* (God). "Big Father has no need for a human father or mother. He has always existed. God is a spirit and doesn't need a body like we do." Potbelly thought that one over for a while before asking "Does he have a head?" At least he was thinking.

The group began visiting our camp on a daily basis. When the men went on an outing with them to fell honey trees with their chainsaws, Alan suggested to Dick, "You should go with me in the *yatsitata* (airplane) to visit your other's camp (the Chimoré). We can cut sugarcane for you to bring back." Dick was receptive to Alan's suggestion, unlike his older brother Tom who continued to resist the idea altogether.

Later the band let us know they were planning on traveling again. Before leaving on their trip though, they invited Alan, Grant Mayer, and two of the Chimoré Yuquí to spend a night near their camp and go hunting for monkeys with them the following morning. Our guys spent the night about fifteen feet from the edge of their camp. When morning came, the nomads invited them into their campsite to warm themselves by their fires. They thought it was hilarious that our men slept with no fire. Sitting next to Tom and Vera, the deceased chief's wife, Alan warmed himself by their fire.

Before long, they left to go hunting. As they followed the river, the young warriors explained they needed to retrieve arrows they had left behind when fleeing from the *abaas* (enemies). They had been hunting monkeys at the time, so the arrows were lodged high up in the trees. After reaching the spot, everyone sat around while Tom sent his slave, Potbelly, up tree after tree to retrieve the large arrows.

Because of the cold, they built a fire and huddled around it while watching Tom's poor slave repeatedly risk his life. One arrow was lodged high up in a big tree whose diameter was too great to shinny up; the main crotch of the tree was over forty feet above ground. Potbelly tried to climb the tree but came back down where he grabbed a thinner sapling, smaller in diameter; then up he went again.

After ascending roughly twenty-five feet, the sapling swayed so vigorously from side to side that Alan thought the tree might snap right in two! Still Potbelly persevered, climbing another eight feet or so. When he got to the highest point he could reach, he seized a large vine from an adjacent towering tree. Utilizing the vine for support, he managed to pull the top of the sapling up against the huge tree and secure it with liana vines, then clambered across.

From there the slave ascended another ten feet until he reached the broad fork of the giant tree.

Having reached the fork, he then shinnied up the massively wide branches hanging on with a tenacious grip. Despite the challenges, the slave persevered, ascending to the tree's upper boughs. There, he shook the limbs until the prized arrow of his master was dislodged and tumbled down to the ground.

Now all Potbelly needed to do was climb back down! After performing this dangerous yet impressive feat, he still had at least three other arrows to retrieve. What a miserable fate to be born a Yuquí slave.

Meanwhile, the group pressed on, stopping occasionally so Vera could peel long strips of bark from *ambaibo* trees. When they stopped to retrieve arrows, she spent the time separating the pliable inner layer of bark from the brittle exterior. She would take the soft material back to camp to dry before shredding it into strips that would be rolled into string for making a hammock, baby sling, or rope for a bow string. The hunting trip was not fruitful, so eventually the group decided to return to their jungle camp.

At the nomad's campsite, Grant Mayer spent his time observing, taking note of the individuals at each fire to discern the family

Matador's son playing with missionary children

groups. Alan took special note as well and together they identified twenty-four individuals forming four primary family units. Vera and Tom, the chief's wife and brother, were accompanied by five boys, all sons of the late chief Matador. Matador's oldest son had often played with our children in camp riding a motorless go-kart. The youngest was Little Turtle (Clubfoot). Friday, as their slave completed the group of eight.

At Dick's fire (Matador's other younger brother), Jane appeared to be his sleeping partner. She sat behind Dick looking very upset. It seemed they weren't on speaking terms. Potbelly, being Dick's slave, was among them. Several children joined them around the fire; one was a very cute little girl we affectionately referred to as Monkey Eyes. Nearby, Tapir's fire was surrounded by young children, with Sunday, presumed to be Tapir's daughter, sitting close by.

Those they considered more expendable sat at another fire: Harry, Spooky, Grandma, and Blanca's two young, orphaned girls. Blanca belonged to the slave class and was one of the twelve missing and presumed dead.

The dynamics of power and servitude were starkly illustrated by Potbelly who seemed to play the role of a dog to his master. Dick sat in his hammock like a king, gorging on food. Tearing apart the head on a piranha, he ate the meat and tossed the sharp bony

A high-class Yuquí couple

skeleton to Potbelly, who squatted on the ground next to him. The slave licked the bones clean and sucked off any edible morsels that were left. Then he was handed the scales of the fish, which he hungrily gobbled down.

Now onto dessert. Having had the good fortune of finding honey, Dick reached over to his big, shiny aluminum kettle that he had traded for a bow and arrow and opened the lid. After grabbing a big chunk of honeycomb, he chewed the sweet nectar from its' cells, enjoying this "drink of the gods". Then he pulled the chewed wax from his mouth and handed it to Potbelly, who chomped on it, hoping for a few drops of honey. It didn't matter to Dick that his slave had suffered numerous thorns and stings to present the honeycomb to his master. Such was the complex social hierarchy and relationships within these small groups of nomadic people.

Potbelly seemed to have resigned himself to the harsh realities of his birth into slavery, a common fate within Yuquí society. Dick's high-class family slept the night in one solitary *ambaibo* bark rope hammock, while Potbelly squatted or lay on the ground throughout the night tending the fire. The wafting smoke would keep the mosquitoes at bay for his master's family. One wonders how this poor slave managed to stay alive.

Tapir, while widowed, appeared to be taken care of and may have been an older sister to Tom and Dick. She had several daughters who could eventually become wives for Matador and Vera's sons. The family group that was neglected was Grandma, slaves Harry and Spooky, and Blanca's two orphaned children. All were suffering from malnutrition.

When it was time for Alan, Grant, and our two Christian Yuquí comrades to return to the Víbora base, Grandma, Harry, and Spooky, with Blanca's two small children, tagged along, planning to spend the night back in our camp. Had the rest of their group allowed it, these mistreated nomads most likely would have moved right into our camp. Our five guests received royal treatment. We hoped when they returned to the others, they could convince the rest of the jungle dwellers to settle down and join their kinfolk at the Chimoré Base. Regrettably, that was not to be. Their visit was the last we saw of the nomads for almost another four months.

The Roaring Lion

Be sober, be vigilant; because your adversary
the devil walks about like a roaring lion, seeking
whom he may devour. 1 Peter 5:8 NKJV

A heavy oppression, one we had not sensed in our previous contacts, pervaded our interactions with the nomads once they returned. Their change of attitude left us mystified. Before their four-month absence, our interactions with them had been very friendly, with both the missionaries and the *Bia* spending a night in each other's camp. Now we sensed a keen hostility. Instead of showing interest in spiritual matters like before, they expressed animosity if God was even mentioned. What had triggered such an extreme change of mindset toward us? Our team, husbands and wives, gathered together for earnest prayer seeking God's wisdom and guidance.

Gleaning from the final chapters of *"Someone Must Die,"* I continue...

We sensed that Satan, described figuratively as *"the prince of the power of the air"* in Ephesians 2:2, had been particularly active during their four-month absence from us. Determined to maintain his hold over this small band, the devil was working hard to lead the bedraggled group astray. Under his influence, the *Bia* had shot four of our men in earlier efforts to befriend them. How we longed to share God's love and the liberating truth of the Gospel with them.

After more than fifty contacts with the hostiles and a budding friendship with them, their band of thirty-six was now reduced to just twenty-four individuals in spite of our continual warnings and pleas not to interfere with the colonists. Not only were they being murdered by nationals, but they killed their very own people, believing Satan's lie that others had to be murdered to accompany the spirits of their ruling-class dead into the next world. At this rate, these few remaining nomads would soon cease to exist on earth.

For you are the children of your father the devil,
and you love to do the evil things he does. He was
a murderer from the beginning. He has always
hated the truth, because there is no truth in him.
When he lies, it is consistent with his character; for
he is a liar and the father of lies. John 8:44 NLT

"Ponder how valuable your soul must be for Satan to
tirelessly pursue it, and the Son of God to lay down
his own life for it." D. L. Moody

Sickness had broken out at the Chimoré base, which hindered our Yuquí comrades from flying over to help us at this time. Despite their absence, many of our interactions with the nomads were friendly and carried on as usual, but at other times our men sensed evil intent on the part of the *Bia,* and the oppression was palpable. In a particularly unsettling incident, things were going along extremely well when Tom's face (the group's young new leader) took on a very disturbing alteration. His facial features twisted and contorted into what Alan could only describe as "an almost nonhuman grimace." Satan's demons were working behind the scenes.

Unbeknownst to the missionaries, the *Bia*'s hostility towards us stemmed from the profound cultural crisis they faced: the loss of their chief and leaders. Evil spiritual forces had convinced the nomads that they had failed to properly honor the spirits of their dead chief and warriors. It

On the right Chief Matador,
who was killed by nationals

was imperative for them to kill additional people to accompany these spirits, or they would suffer dire consequences. With their numbers already dwindled to just twenty-four, the dilemma of killing more people left them overwhelmed. Satan's yoke was heavy indeed; if they didn't kill others, they themselves might suffer dire consequences. But who could they kill to satisfy these spirits? Their band was already severely reduced in number; killing more of their own was an unacceptable solution.

Those of us at the Víbora persevered at gathering together for times of earnest prayer. While some nomads appeared genuinely pleased with the missionaries' presence, others were less welcoming. We were the first outsiders to show empathy and sincere concern for their welfare, a friendship they not only wanted but needed for their own survival. But something was terribly wrong. "Perhaps we are pushing them too hard, " Alan remarked. "They are beginning to resist, and we need to back off for a while."

It wasn't until much later that we learned the nomads were searching for their "real fathers" during their absences. Their "real fathers" were a group they had split away from shortly before their initial encounters with us. They were also searching for the bodies of their missing dead and had recovered at least three, the chief's body being one of them. Of course, we had no way of knowing this.

Tom and Dick couldn't provide adequate meat for the entire band of twenty-four with their key hunters gone. On top of this, they felt overcome with the pressing need to appease the spirits of their dead.

They left one day saying they would return in two days but didn't show up. As the team sought the Lord in prayer, they felt that a small crew of three guys should hike to the Chore River to see if the nomads had camped there. If so, the men would camp nearby but not too close. They wanted to make themselves available and hoped to encourage the *Bia* to return to our camp once again.

The following day, Steve Parker, Félix Ovales (a national comrade), and Alan went out to the Chore River where the nomads had frequently camped and met with us. After crossing the river, the guys hooted loudly to alert the *Bia* of their arrival. No response. They continued hiking and hooting, again with no response from the *Bia*, so our men returned to their campsite to sleep the night there.

Felix, Alan, and Steve
heading to the jungle

They resumed hiking through the jungle the next day and came across a recently abandoned nomad camp as well as the trail the nomads had taken upon leaving. The men returned to their campsite and prayed again for guidance, then discussed what they should do next. Alan had hesitations about pursuing them, but the other two men were confident they should continue searching, so Alan consented. Now they just needed to turn on their Stoner transceiver and update those of us back at the Víbora camp via radio.

"We've found their campsite and trail and are planning to follow them. We'll keep you informed as we are able."

"Understood," came the reply, "we'll be praying for you."

At the Víbora base, I felt a strong premonition that our men would be shot if they continued trailing the *Bia*. I shared my concerns with Larry Depue, who was managing the radio. "The nomads have a great respect for the guns our men are carrying," he reassured me. Though the team would never shoot to kill them, they certainly would shoot to scare the warriors away in dangerous situations.

Back in the jungle, Steve, Félix, and Alan disconnected the radio gear and distributed the various components among the three of them so no one pack would be too heavy, then they headed out. Concern for the nomads weighed heavily on their hearts knowing that if they couldn't convince them to move to the Chimoré, they most likely would not survive.

The Lord led our men down nearly invisible paths as they hiked for six hard hours. Parts of the jungle were more spacious, but a lot of it was filled with dense thorns and underbrush that tore at their clothing and skin. It was nearly impossible to travel through these parts of the rainforest. The occasional ravine meant the three men slid and crawled down steep walls and gullies and tried to find a way up the other side by holding onto roots and vines, all the while carrying a fifty-pound backpack with a rifle in one hand and a machete to cut through vines in the other.

By one o'clock, they all had reached their limit, when in God's providence, they stumbled upon the camp where the nomads had spent the previous night. Coals from their fires were still hot. Evidently, the *Bia* had taken off only a few hours earlier, so they couldn't be far ahead.

Steve, Félix, and Alan ate some lunch and rested to gain back some strength. Taking off again, they hoped they might encounter the nomads as they were setting up their next camp. The plan worked well. Alan had given young domestic piglets to the leaders of the group on previous contacts and the piglets followed their owners through the jungle much like a pet dog. After losing the trail, tracks of the piglets were found, enabling the team to continue ahead. Pieces of palm branches from which they had woven their packs, as well as ashes dropped from the smoldering embers they carried, also gave clear indication that our men were right on their trail. With so many obvious signs, the men were sure the nomad's camp wasn't far.

"If we get near them, why don't you let me go first?" Alan quietly suggested to Félix who was leading the way.

"I had that in mind," Félix responded.

Soon, Félix stopped and motioned for Alan to take the lead; they had come upon a palm-thatched hut. What they didn't realize was that they were closing in on the nomad's camp. Advancing a short distance, they discovered two more thatched huts. It wasn't until later that our men realized the palm-thatched huts were burial shelters for the bodies of their missing men, which the *Bia* had recovered.

Alan decided to whistle like the Yuquí typically do when returning from a hunt. They signal their approach by drawing in air and whistling a low tone that gradually ascends higher, thus notifying the people in camp that one of their own is approaching and not an *abaa* (enemy). He expected someone to respond with two short indrawn whistles. Instead, a woman's frightened cry echoed back. Our men had caught the nomads totally unawares.

"It's me! It's me!" Alan cried out in dialect. "It's us! It's us!" and without waiting for a reply, the guys pushed forward.

Suddenly, they found themselves in a clearing near the two burial huts and were immediately joined by a small group of the nomads. In the past, their warriors all showed up armed with bow and arrows and a worried look on their faces when our men met them in the jungle. Not this time. They approached the guys empty-handed with smiling faces, expressing great delight at seeing them again. Even though the abrupt entrance had alarmed some, they still came running over as if to say, "Hey, it's sure great to see you again!"

After a few moments, the two leaders, Tom and Dick, showed up with their weapons in hand but not in a threatening way. Our men still wondered what the two huts were for and within the hour, received the answer to their question.

"That's Papa's house," Vera stated as she pointed to one of the shelters. She repeated this several times to make sure the guys clearly understood it was Matador's burial shelter, her husband and former chief, the one she had so deeply mourned for. Likely, his decaying body was inside the shelter wrapped in woven palm mats and lying on a raised platform. They would leave the body there until the flesh rotted from the bones and then repackage the bones in fresh mats. Eventually, the bones would be placed in a palm leaf basket and carried with them in their jungle wanderings.

A dead Yuquí's bones inside the shelter

Later, Alan learned the nomads were in the process of "renewing the bones," repackaging them, and moving them to new shelters which had already been constructed beyond their camp.

The *Bia* seemed to have no problem with our men being in their camp. After visiting, they encouraged the three men to set up camp for the night. There was some discourse about where our guys should camp. Most of the group appeared to be content with Steve, Félix, and Alan just sleeping right among the nomads' own campsite. It was pretty clear though, that Tom, the older of the two young leaders, resisted that idea, so, our guys camped just a short distance down the trail but still close enough to see the smoke from the nomad's fires.

As our men were finishing setting up, Friday, one of the slaves, meandered over and remarked, "We lost a knife here. Let's look for the knife." The jungle floor was covered with dry brittle leaves to a depth of at least six inches. Soon, Friday was joined by some of the others who started pushing leaves here and there as they searched, ostensibly for a knife. In the process, they cleared two smooth trails.

By now, Alan was lying on the ground in his jungle hammock and Steve in a portable tent. Our national coworker Félix slept on the ground under a mosquito net. Alan hadn't paid much attention to the nomads searching for the knife, but once he climbed into his hammock, his weary mind instantly became alert.

"Steve, they aren't looking for a knife. They're clearing trails so they won't tread on dry leaves when they come back to shoot us in the night!"

When the nomads had finished sweeping through the dry leaves with their hands, one of them asked, "Hey, do you have those things you shine at night to see tapirs?" (referring to flashlights).

"We sure do." It was getting dark, and the three men pulled out their flashlights and turned them on. Alan remarked, "See how bright they shine!"

The nomads watched as the men shone their lights all around the area, taking special note to illuminate the guns that each of them had next to them in their individual beds. The *Bia* had hunted enough with our men to know how proficient each of them was using their weapons. Alan and the nomads bantered back and forth a bit before he jokingly said, "After you all go to bed, we're going to move camp. Since we have lights, we are going to move to where you can't find us." The night was dark, and the full moon wouldn't be up until almost morning.

The *Bia*'s apparent plans to shoot our fellas in the night were aborted as they realized our guys had the advantage with their flashlights and guns.

Dick, Tom's younger brother, asked, "Did you bring your fishing lines?" Once he was assured our men had lines, Dick proposed, "Let's go fishing for pacú (large sunfish) tomorrow. The river isn't far from us."

With that, they left, and our men lay down to get some much-needed rest, but not before Alan asked Steve and Félix, "Shall we set a guard?" It was decided that all three would remain alert until it grew very dark. They managed to catch a brief period of sleep, yet in the wee hours, with the ascent of the moon casting its glow, they remained vigilant. Knowing their lives were on the line, none of them had trouble waking when the moon began lighting the sky.

Ambushed

As dawn broke, Tom, Dick, Potbelly, and Harry were eager to join our men for a fishing trip. Steve considered bringing the bulky radio gear to get in touch with the spouses at the Víbora base during the outing; however, the nomads assured the guys that the river was close by and they could easily return after fishing. Opting to communicate with their wives upon their return, the men set off for the river without the radio.

En route, the warriors changed their minds and suggested hunting monkeys instead, telling the missionaries to leave their fishing gear along the path. Shortly into their trek, they heard a troop of monkeys jumping through the trees. Monkeys were easy game to shoot and prized among the nomads, but Tom and Dick decided not to hunt and appeared moody and out of sorts. Heightened with a sense of unease, our men decided to head back to their camp to alert the rest of us at the Víbora base.

Félix, leading the way, and now wary of the warriors' intentions, pretended to lose the path, feigning he couldn't find the trail. When he suggested the *Bia* take the lead, Tom and Dick angrily insisted he continue at the front. With no other option, Félix resumed his position, followed by Steve, Alan, and the four armed and sullen warriors in a tense procession.

Our men heightened their alertness to an extreme degree, a state that inevitably led to fatigue. Eventually, Steve, weary with the constant vigilance, decided to place his faith in divine protection for any threats that might come from behind and prayed, "Father, I'm entrusting my back into your care," then proceeded to bend over as he stepped over some slippery tree roots.

The harsh sound of an arrow grating its way across a palmwood bow brought an instant reaction from Alan, and he found he had thrown himself to the ground on his right while pivoting 180 degrees. Hearing the dull thud of an arrow driving deep into Steve's back, he fired four quick shots over the attackers. Along with all of this was the sound of air being violently expelled from Steve's lungs and an agonized groan as the arrow impacted. In Alan's heightened sense of awareness, he took in the entire scene with just a glance. Potbelly had a fully drawn bow with an eight-foot arrow aimed right at Félix, who was crouched over and turning to his right.

With his gun still aimed down the back trail, Alan released two quick shots above Potbelly. His first four shots were just a triggered reaction, but the last two were fired with an ATTITUDE! The missionary team had sacrificed so much to save these jungle dwellers, and *this* was how they were repaying our kindness! Alan's shots startled the attackers who screamed with terror. Two dropped their weapons as all four fled.

As quickly as the attack had begun, it was over. Of the four attackers, the image seared into Alan's mind was of Potbelly with a fully drawn bow following Félix's movement to get a shot at him. Alan's two shots along with Félix's movement had caused Potbelly to miss.

Our missionary team had interacted with the nomads over the course of several years, hunted together with them numerous times, constantly invited them into our camp, all the while cooking up kettles of rice and corn and providing them with an endless supply of meat and bananas. Why? Why, after almost sixty contacts and their growing trust in our friendship and protection, would they turn on us like this? Why had they tried to kill Alan's two colleagues?

Both Steve and Felix had been hit by bleeder-tipped arrows, with Felix only slightly wounded since the arrow ricocheted off his left shoulder blade; however, Steve lay on the ground where he had fallen. A lance-shaped, bleeder-tipped arrow had entered low on the right side of his back and the tip had driven itself all the way through his body and now protruded from his chest. The bamboo tip itself was two inches wide and roughly eighteen inches long, creating a wide semicircular incision where it had entered. With the arrow shaft broken off, only the tip ends protruded from his back and chest. Steve's moaning broke the silence, "Pull it out, brother. It hurts!"

Though greatly distressed at seeing Steve's agony, Alan responded, "I can't pull it out. We need to leave it in, or you will bleed to death." In my husband's younger years growing up in the small jungle town of Todos Santos, he recalled witnessing at least one man die after being shot with a bleeder-tipped arrow. The doctors in Cochabamba had stated, "If the local doctor had left the arrow tip in the wound, the man would have survived." Alan had determined then and there, at the tender age of twelve, that if he ever faced a similar situation, he would not pull the arrow out.

The three men huddled together tightly in a slight depression on the jungle floor with a fallen log and some trees around them. Alan and Félix were still holding their guns, with each watching 180 degrees in opposite directions, listening carefully in case of another attack.

Once they were convinced the Yuquí had fled, Steve said, "Go for the radio, brother."

Deeply concerned, Alan responded, "I'll go, but it won't be there. By now, the *Bia* have stolen all our belongings, but at least I can go back to look and retrieve what is possible, but let's pray first." His knees trembled so badly he could hardly stand up.

Following their prayers, Alan stood up and tried to head off to their previous night's campsite, but his legs shook so violently that they barely held him up, and he felt his stomach churn ominously. Acknowledging the trauma had left him in a state of shock, he knew he wouldn't get very far and pivoted back to his companions.

"Brothers, we need to pray again." So they prayed once more, committing Steve and Félix to the Lord and Alan to God's care. He rose and headed back to the campsite, which was twenty to thirty minutes away. Having left the radio equipment in their backpacks, he had little hope of finding it there. No doubt the warriors had taken what they could use and thrown the rest away where the men would never find it. With Steve vitally wounded and lying defenseless on the ground, Félix remained by his side. This left Alan to navigate the barely trodden path alone alone but with God.

Alan repeated that refrain multiple times to himself, *Alone... with God! Alone... with God!* As he ventured into the unknown, he clung to the mantra, *Alone... with God!* Despite his doubts about retracing the faint trail, the urgency of Steve's precarious state propelled him forward without delay.

As he stumbled through dense jungle, he often lost the trail. When he couldn't find it again, he prayed for God's help and invariably found himself back on track. How grateful he was to have a Divine Guide showing him the way. The nomads might very well be waiting in ambush, anticipating our men would return for their packs. With each step, Alan considered potential sites where the *Bia* might be hiding to make their attack. He had a keen sense of direction after living so long in the jungle; even so, the trail was practically impossible to follow with only an occasional bent or broken twig to mark it.

> *Your ears shall hear a word behind you, saying,*
> *"This is the way, walk in it...,"* Isaiah 30:21 NKJV

With the heavy sense of danger and urgency, the campsite seemed much farther away than it actually was. After some time, Alan began to recognize the area and knew he was less than a hundred yards from last night's campsite. This was also the most likely point for another ambush. If the warriors were lying in wait, they would expect our guys to return to this spot for their belongings.

He decided the quickest and safest method to reach the campsite was to dash across the open stretch of jungle. Unencumbered by a backpack, he raced toward a massive tree with large fins rising from the ground, which promised him shelter. Reaching the tree, he positioned himself so the fins shielded him from both sides, leaving only a 120-degree frontal arc exposed to potential threats. This strategic spot provided Alan a fighting chance for survival, thanks to the clear line of sight it offered.

Having been so consumed with trying to build a friendship with the *Bia*, he chastised himself for not recognizing the seriousness of their malicious intent earlier. Having spent fifteen years deeply engaged in the Yuquí culture and language, and regularly joining them in hunting throughout the years, Alan chided himself for his lack of insight. The hostiles had embraced him, believing him to be reincarnated kin, forging a strong connection. However, even the loss of their prominent warriors to colonists or loggers had not fully alerted him to the danger his team faced.

Leaning against the massive tree, he surveyed the area and, with newfound insight, pieced together the sequence of events leading up to Steve being shot. The day before, prior to reaching the nomad's encampment, Steve, Félix, and Alan had stumbled upon a clearing strewn with damaged aluminum kettles and shattered glass bottles—items the nomads typically treasured but now were discarded or destroyed. Then they had come upon the burial huts, one of which held the decaying body of their beloved chief. Circumstances Alan hadn't fully comprehended before became crystal clear.

All the items that were abandoned or destroyed had been sacrificed to the spirits of their dead, and the missionaries had failed to attach an adequate level of importance to what they had seen. Then there was the night before, when the nomads were clearing leaves around our men's campsite. The pieces of the puzzle were all falling in place now. With the *Bia*'s numbers dwindling to just twenty-four, the tribe needed every member to ensure their survival. This raised the haunting question: Who could be spared to join the spirits in the afterlife? As much as they longed for our friendship, provisions, and care, the nomads couldn't sacrifice one of their own; even their slaves were too precious to lose.

As Alan pondered these revelations, his mind returned to the task at hand. Steve needed help and he needed it now! With no visible threat of arrows, his priority was clear: Steve's life hung in the balance!

After looking around, he discovered most of the men's gear had vanished just as he had anticipated. Steve and Felix's packs had disappeared, as well as the cooking kettles, the canteens full of water, and the machetes; all of it had been taken... but God! God had seen to it that Alan's pack had been left behind, untouched. Evidently, the nomads were trying to keep on his good side, possibly hoping they could return to our Víbora camp at some future time.

Steve and Félix's packs had contained much of the essential radio equipment, such as the transceiver, microphone, and antenna. One of them also held the battery pack. Without these, sending a distress call to our Víbora base was out of the question.

God had prompted Steve and Félix to pull the radio gear out of their packs before heading out on the morning fishing expedition, while my husband had kept his portion secured in his backpack. Alan saw that Steve and Félix's packs were gone, along with any hope of calling for help. A wave of relief washed over him as he spotted all the radio gear sitting on the ground near his own backpack. Overcome with joy and gratitude, he praised and thanked God for keeping all the radio gear intact.

Hastily, he retrieved the 116-foot dipole antenna from his pack. Knowing time was of the essence, he opted not to meticulously arrange the antenna through the trees. Instead, he tossed one end over some nearby shrubbery as far as possible, then did the same with the other end in the opposite direction. With the connector fastened to the back of the radio, the antenna setup was complete. He plugged the microphone in, screwed on the battery cables using his Swiss Army knife, and then powered it on.

A burst of static filled the air as the radio came to life. He pressed the microphone button and urgently called, "Emergency, emergency! This is Chore River with an emergency. Are you there Víbora?"

Immediately, Larry Depue at the Víbora Base responded, "What's the problem, Chore River?"

"We've been attacked. Steve is hit hard. We need help immediately!"

Larry gathered more details about their situation and sprang into action, then immediately informed me and Steve's wife, Vangie, of the ambush. Without delay, he began coordinating the search for a helicopter and planes to aid in the rescue operation. A ground crew would be needed that could be dropped at the nearest beach on the Chore River. From there, the crew would need to cut their way through the jungle to where Steve lay struggling for his life. Fortunately, Alan's Vietnam-era army surplus hammock had loops along the side where poles could be inserted to repurpose the hammock into a stretcher so Steve could be carried to the beach.

Alan informed Larry that he was in the process of packing up the radio equipment and would be off the air while he made his way back down the trail to where Steve and Félix awaited. He rolled up his jungle hammock and took it along so Steve would have some protection from the myriads of jungle insects. Moments later, he was on his way, confident not only in Larry's abilities but the commitment of the missionary team in Bolivia as well as the prayers of Christians worldwide. There is a tremendous sense of united love among God's people and our mission community. Within minutes, word was going out worldwide by radio, asking for prayer. Our pilot and pilots from other missions were dropping everything to lend a hand as God drew together a team to rescue his wounded children.

As he headed back to where Steve and Félix waited, Alan was grateful for the protection the pack on his back gave from arrows that potentially could be shot from behind.

Upon his arrival, he found Steve lying in the same spot where he had collapsed. By that time, Steve had broken off the arrow's shaft protruding from his back but left the bamboo point embedded. The Yuquí bleeder tips were designed to bring down formidable creatures such as jaguars and tapirs and were always used with lethal intent. Despite the blood-soaked earth, Steve had moved very little and the broad point in his back helped stem the bleeding. Félix did his utmost to alleviate Steve's discomfort. Meanwhile, Alan arranged his jungle hammock, offering Steve some protection against the voracious mosquitoes.

Again, my husband contacted the Víbora River base via radio. A South American Mission pilot, Tom Bush, was already in the air to locate them and help guide the helicopter and rescue team into the site. The jungle here was marked by lofty trees and moderate undergrowth, not as impenetrable as some areas of the rainforest. If Steve couldn't be carried out to a beach, a significant clearing would need to be done before a helicopter could land amidst these massive trees.

Trouble at the Víbora

Malevolent spiritual forces were not only hindering our men's efforts in the jungle but also obstructing any attempts from the Vibora to reach Steve. A helicopter had landed at our jungle airstrip with a volunteer rescue team onboard. Coworkers, Larry Depue and Jack Jones, had just climbed on board to join the team. The crew planned to set off immediately for a beach near where Steve had been shot.

However, the weather was deteriorating rapidly with ominous black clouds rolling in, creating a sense of urgency. The chopper needed to take off right away. As the mighty rotor blades fired up, the roar resonated through camp and we all expected an imminent departure. Unexpectedly, the blades came to an abrupt standstill; the chopper had blown a fuse. The pilot climbed out, replaced the fuse, and started the aircraft up once more only to have the fuse blow again. With black clouds rolling in, it was paramount to get the aircraft off the ground as quickly as possible, but the fuse continued giving problems.

Meanwhile, across the river in our camp, a novice missionary had stayed behind to watch over the wives and children. Peering out my window, I noticed him standing in the aluminum boat, preparing to start the gas-powered outboard motor. He was heading to the other side of the river to see what was going on with the chopper. Being unaware that the outboard had been modified by its owner to bypass the safety mechanism which normally prevented it from starting in gear, he started the motor. As erratic "WHUMPA, WHUMPA, WHUMPAS" from the helicopter's failed attempts echoed in the distance, the roar of a motorboat resounding at full throttle signaled trouble on our side of the river.

The unexpected takeoff thrust the new missionary right out of the boat, and I watched in horror as the boat spun in circles around him. He could have been chopped to pieces! Bolting out the door, I dashed across camp shouting, "Man overboard!" as his wife simultaneously tore out of her house to rescue him. The whole situation was so absurd, I almost laughed out loud just to keep from crying. What more could possibly go wrong!

As if on cue, a deafening "WHUMPA, WHUMPA, WHUMPA" roaring overhead signaled the helicopter was finally airborne, leaving behind some very frazzled missionary wives as the empty boat spun around the only man left in camp. After a harrowing ordeal, the badly bruised missionary was finally rescued, once the runaway boat, starved of fuel, eventually sputtered to a stop.

Meanwhile, back in the jungle, Alan had paced away from where Steve lay injured, to the spot where he had witnessed Potbelly aiming his arrow at Félix. There, discarded by the retreating nomads, were two hefty bows and a quartet of arrows. In the Yuquí culture, snapping a fellow warrior's arrows was a potent display of anger. For weightier offenses, they would break the bow itself. Wanting to communicate to the *Bia* his outrage for shooting his beloved coworkers, Alan located two trees close together and levered the thick palm-wood bows until they finally broke. He then shattered the arrows into many unrepairable pieces and arranged the fragments on the nomads' path as a stark message. In time, the warriors would return for their weaponry, discover the splintered shards, and understand the depth of Alan's anger.

As the hours dragged on, Alan administered the few oral painkillers he had to Steve, while Félix tirelessly swatted away insects and fanned the oppressive heat from their grievously wounded coworker. Options exhausted, they could only wait as the seconds stretched into hours.

Suddenly, a distant thrum pierced the silence—the helicopter blades cleaving the air, a very welcome announcement as it descended onto the riverbank only a mile away. To Steve, the sound was music to his ears. The rescue team had been dispatched to a river bank a mere two thousand yards from Steve's location. The crew expected to reach him by one o'clock that afternoon.

The rescue craft

What Steve didn't realize was that his faith would be extremely tested while spending a tortuous night on the dense jungle floor before the rescue team could even reach him. The tangled undergrowth near the Chore River beach was so formidable, the crew advanced a mere 150 yards after 90 minutes of exhausting work. Even though the work was daunting, the men persevered to clear a path wide enough for a stretcher; however, the trail was littered with debris, complicating their progress.

In the meantime, Steve endured unbearable pain; the bleeder tip made each breath agonizing. He felt death was imminent. In spite of the excruciating pain, he had complete assurance that his sins were forgiven, and death would only usher him into the glorious presence of his Savior and Lord. Nevertheless, Steve didn't want to leave his wife, Vangie, and their six children alone.

Do not be afraid of those who kill the
body but cannot kill the soul.
Rather, be afraid of the One who can destroy both
soul and body in hell. Matthew 10:28 NIV

"My purpose in writing is simply this: that you
who believe in God's Son will know beyond the
shadow of a doubt that you have eternal life, the
reality and not the illusion." 1 John 5:13 MSG

As time ticked away with no rescuers in sight, at two o'clock the decision was made for Alan to hike toward the Chore River at a bearing of 280 degrees, with the hope of intercepting the rescue team and expediting their journey to Steve. Equipped with the compass heading thanks to the air crew, Alan set off, armed with just his rifle, having left behind his pack and flashlight for Steve and Félix. All of their machetes had been stolen by their attackers.

Eventually, he crossed a narrow, shallow waterway, where he drank water to his fill, and whispered gratitude to his Heavenly Father for quenching his thirst. Further on, he found himself in a vast dry swamp with vegetation so thick he had to crawl through on his hands and knees. Without the aid of a machete, Alan was reduced to kneeling on the ground, pushing the dense undergrowth apart, throwing his gun through the opening and crawling through. The process had to be repeated over and over and over again.

At one point, he climbed a tree, hoping to get some indication that he was near the river. All he could see was a thick, dry swamp for what looked like miles around, an extremely demoralizing discovery! *The river's got to be ahead if I just keep going west,* he reasoned and pressed on.

The unbearable heat and strenuous exertion had completely depleted his body of water. All his clothing was soaked, so much so that it looked like he had just climbed out of the river. Time and again, Alan collapsed from sheer exhaustion. By five o'clock, with his strength gone, he knew he couldn't arrive at the river before nightfall.

Meanwhile, back at our Víbora camp, the women, children, and a very bruised male missionary hunkered down for the night. I stayed with Steve's wife, Vangie, to offer support. Both of us were weighed down by the grim thought of Steve enduring the night on the jungle floor, impaled by a Yuquí arrow. Our older children, Sammy and Becky, were at boarding school at this time. However, our youngest, five-year-old Caleb, was with us and was delighted at having a sleepover with his best friend Stevie, both unaware of the peril their fathers faced deep in the jungle.

Even though I knew Alan would spend the night isolated in the wild, I was enveloped by an extraordinary peace. His extensive experience in traveling the jungle alongside the Yuquí, coupled with his sharp navigational skills, comforted me. Yet it was the profound conviction that God's presence was right there with him, that instilled such serenity. Vangie, too, demonstrated a serene trust in God, certain that He was with Steve during the ordeal. God's palpable presence was providing us all with strength, comfort, and assurance.

You will keep in perfect peace those whose minds are steadfast, because they trust in You. Isaiah 26:3 NIV

He Giveth More Grace

Before nightfall, Alan had spotted a massive, uprooted tree; its enormous roots formed a shelter resembling a dome-shaped cave. After gathering some decaying timber and dry leaves, he succeeded in kindling a fire. The rising warmth began to evaporate the moisture from his soaked garments as the heat reflected off the large root behind him. Exhausted to his core, he could barely muster a whisper with his throat so extremely parched.

Suddenly, a distant hoot pierced the silence, followed by the echo of gunfire. Though it sounded far away, the rescue team was actually a mere hundred yards from him, their proximity disguised by the night's misleading breeze. Despite his exhaustion, Alan attempted a response, but his feeble raspy hoot was lost in the wind. As darkness enveloped him, the sanctuary of the tree roots was too precious to abandon. The fire glowed against the back wall and there were few mosquitoes. He thanked his Heavenly Father for directing him to safe shelter; water was the only thing he lacked. With the rescue team so close, a comforting fire, and a loaded gun, Alan's thoughts turned to Steve. He was convinced God was in control of the whole situation and prayed for sustaining strength for Steve.

Throughout that day and night, Steve found himself enrolled in the school of faith. When he had committed the watchkeeping of his back to God, he had meant, "Don't let it be shot with an arrow." Now, with a broken arrow shaft jutting from his back and the bleeder tip protruding from his chest, he wondered, *Had God failed Him?*

Another big difficulty was that Steve was very dehydrated. His throat was so parched it stuck together, triggering an uncontrollable desire to heave. He and Félix had no water, but they prayed, and others were praying for them. During the night, the unmistakable sound of pitter-patter announced a light rain was falling.

Félix, who himself was wounded in the shoulder, found a small measure of relief for Steve by crawling around on his hands and knees with a flashlight to look for droplets of water collected in leaves on the forest floor. It was tedious, but the moisture would open Steve's throat for about an hour. A number of times, Steve asked Félix to pray, thinking he might not have strength to survive the night. God heard their prayers. In no way had He forgotten or forsaken His wounded servants.

Early the next morning, the rescue team was up and cutting a trail once again. Alan was already making his way in their direction through the dense undergrowth. This time when the crew hooted, he was able to respond though barely, since his throat was still very parched. He fired his rifle to give the crew a clearer indication of where he was.

By six o'clock that morning Alan had joined forces with the squad of six men, two being Yuquí friends from the Chimoré base. Still being a good distance away from Steve, Alan told them they needed to follow a heading of one hundred degrees, the reciprocal of what he had traveled to meet them. A short time later the pilot, Tom Bush, flew over in a small Cessna and circled until our men were able to build a smokey fire. After the pilot located them, he flew back over the crew to give a direct heading to where Steve lay. Off they went with Wooly Hair leading the way. Alan was right behind his Yuquí comrade with a compass while the rest of the crew followed behind. They pushed hard, cutting and pushing their way through the thick brush, giving their all to rescue Steve.

As they continued chopping through dense undergrowth, Alan remarked, "There's just no way Steve will survive if he has to be carried out to the beach through this terrain." Agreeing, the team decided they would clear an area next to Steve so the helicopter could land and get him out. Since Steve was encircled by lofty trees and dense underbrush, Larry Depue proposed having chainsaws lowered by rope to speed up the clearing process.

Relentless hacking continued for over an hour and a half, and Alan knew they were getting close. One of them fired a gun twice. Those gunshots were music to Steve and Félix's ears and Félix fired his gun as a response. The rescue team grinned at each other and headed for the sound of the gunshots.

They arrived at the site by 7:30 a.m. One of the rescue crew, Sam Major, who was a well-trained paramedic, evaluated Steve's condition and administered an IV immediately. The life-giving fluid revived Steve's parched body as well as his spirit.

"He'll Make a Way" by the Crabb family

...He'll make a way in the middle of nowhere...
When it seems no one really cares, He is there by
your side. He'll make a way when you feel Satan
close in. He'll make a way right on time.

A Daring Rescue

"We need a pair of chainsaws, fuel mix, a sharpening file, and an arsenal of axes and machetes," Larry's voice crackled over the radio to his wife at the Víbora, orchestrating a daring operation to carve out a landing zone for the helicopter. "We won't be carrying Steve to the riverbank, over."

"Loud and clear, Chore," Linda's voice echoed back. "We'll get right on that."

"They'll need a long rope for lowering the items," Larry added, "one that can rival trees reaching 120-feet tall or more."

"Affirmative, Chore. We'll let you know when the chopper is heading your way. Flight preparations are in full swing," Linda confirmed, her words a beacon of reassurance. "Tom says to make a smokey fire so the helicopter can spot you."

"Understood, we'll have a signal fire rising, over," Larry affirmed, ready to indicate their position to the skies.

It wasn't long before the chopper's powerful blades were thundering overhead and equipment descended on ropes to the team waiting below. Laboring for hours, the crew cleared a sufficient area of trees to accommodate the helicopter rotors, a herculean task that left a mountain of debris amassed on the jungle floor. The aircraft would have to hover over three or four feet of brush while getting Steve into the chopper. Yet one towering tree, defiant with its overhanging branches, stood tall. The chainsaws had become too dull to fell this final obstacle and our men hoped the helicopter could maneuver around the branches.

The thunderous rhythm of "WHUMPA, WHUMPA, WHUMPA" echoed above as the helicopter surveyed the clearing. Then the pilot's decisive voice crackled over the radio, "That big tree has to go!" The towering giant, almost five feet in diameter, stood as a testament to time, but now time was of the essence. The crew doubted they could resharpen their saws and cut it down before nightfall. With this setback, they wouldn't be able to get Steve into the chopper before darkness fell. Their hearts sank. There was just no way Steve could survive another night on the jungle floor.

In the midst of their exhaustion and deliberations of what to do next, the sudden roar of the helicopter blades slicing through the air completely caught them off guard. In astonishment, they watched the chopper make its descent into the cramped clearing, the pilot expertly maneuvering the craft to dodge the encroaching branches. In a moment, the helicopter was poised directly over the brush pile, but Steve was not on the stretcher, ready for evacuation. "Hurry, hurry with Steve!" was the message shouted to them over the roar of the helicopter.

They rushed over to lift Steve onto the stretcher, an excruciating procedure for our wounded comrade who groaned helplessly. Carefully, they slid him crossways into the hovering chopper. Félix immediately jumped in after him and up they went. The image of Steve being airlifted from that cramped clearing was a poignant reminder of the gravity of their situation.

Taking Steve to the helicopter

The aircraft lifted skyward, but suddenly a jarring thud resounded as a blade struck one of the larger branches of the standing tree. Alan flinched and watched with dismay as the chopper fell to the left. Remarkably, the pilot was able to correct its course and the helicopter ascended into the blue sky above. Their destination was clear: the Víbora base awaited their return.

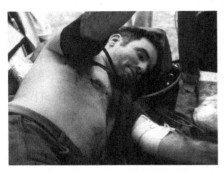

Steve...notice bleeder arrow tip protruding under his lifted arm

Upon Steve's arrival at the base, he was swiftly relocated to the mission's Piper Aztec plane for his flight to Santa Cruz. Within an hour, he would be in the care of medical professionals, addressing his critical needs. Meanwhile, a radio transmission broke the silence: "Chore River, this is Víbora."

The response was prompt: "Roger, Roger, this is the Chore."

"We have disappointing news, Chore. The helicopter pilot says he will not go back in again. You will need to hike home, over."

Despite the setback, spirits were high with the sheer relief of knowing Steve was on his way to the hospital. The men prepared for the arduous return trek, even though it meant another night in the jungle. They gathered all the nonessential gear and piled it on the pool of blood where Steve had lain for the past thirty hours, not wanting to weigh down their packs. Pouring the leftover gasoline mixture from the chain saws over the pile, they set it ablaze to ensure the warriors would not have the pleasure of seeing evidence of the destruction they had wrought. Wooden ax handles were thrown onto the fire and the ax heads were deposited deep into a cavernous tree hollow. They knew the *Bia* would be back to check on the mayhem they had wrought and wanted to ensure their treachery would not be rewarded.

About the time they were ready to head out, the Piper Aztec transporting Steve flew overhead and started circling over their tiny clearing. "He wants us on the radio," Larry said, so they dug the gear back out of their packs to assemble it.

Chuck Henson, our mission pilot, reported, "If you can be at the beach in two hours, the helicopter will pick you up there."

Hurriedly, they repacked and hightailed it to the beach, once again thankful for the Yuquí guides leading the way through the jungle over the rustic trail they had made to reach Steve. Once on the beach, they set up the radio equipment yet again.

"Chore River, Chore River, do you copy?" Another disheartening message was delivered from the Víbora base. The helicopter had a malfunction which would delay their rescue until the following day.

Bad news, good news, and then bad news again! Nevertheless, our guys sensed such relief that Steve had been rescued, the fact that they might have to spend a few more nights in the jungle mattered little to them. Exhausted and famished, since they had carried little food, they opted to go fishing. After setting up camp on the beach, they headed off on a fishing expedition. It wasn't long before they returned to camp empty handed, and that's when they heard it!

The rhythmic pounding of helicopter blades cut through the heavy air, reviving their spirits. In a frantic dash, they returned to their makeshift camp on the beach and reached it just as the helicopter touched down on the sandy shore. The rotorcraft idled, its pilot signaling for four individuals to board. Upon noticing a fifth person, my husband, he shouted for him to join them.

Larry was at the jungle perimeter, dismantling their camp. Alan was unwilling to abandon Larry, so rushed over to help. They had just enough time to pack up before the helicopter returned to evacuate them as well. Once onboard, they conveyed their deep gratitude to the pilot, whose commitment to assist in the emergency was clear.

He went above and beyond, even taking additional risks to ensure Steve was rescued.

Later, in the city, the surgeons in Santa Cruz were filled with wonder. "An absolute miracle!" the doctors exclaimed after a three-hour surgery. They were astounded that an arrow point of such magnitude could traverse a person's torso without piercing any critical blood vessels or organs. Just after Steve had committed his back to the Lord's keeping, he had bent downwards to step over some slippery roots. Then WHAMMO! The arrow impacted him from behind with such force it threw him to the ground. Incredibly, Steve was bending at precisely the perfect incline for the large bleeder tip to pierce his back without hitting vital organs. Only God! Remarkably, even the maggots that had been gnawing in his wound as he lay on the jungle floor were for his benefit. By clearing away the decaying flesh, the maggots had reduced the chance of gangrene setting in.

A few weeks later, we received a note from Steve who was recuperating in the city. "Don't expect me back to the Víbora River base for six to eight weeks, but after that you can expect to see me there!"

Following the traumatic ordeal, my husband settled back into the routine at our Víbora River base and found solace meditating on God's Word. The Lord gave him special encouragement as he meditated on Psalms 27:13–14 KJV:

I had fainted, unless I had believed to see the goodness of the Lord in the land of the living. Wait (with expectation) on the Lord: be of good courage, and He shall strengthen thine heart: wait (expectantly), I say, on the Lord.

Steve, Félix, and Alan were very grateful to still be in *"the land of the living"* and would *"wait expectantly"* for God to work. The assurance in Romans 8:28 NIV also gave special comfort to all of us.

*And we know that in all things God works for
the good of those who love Him, who have
been called according to His purpose.*

God wasn't finished with the nomads yet and we knew it! Alan was
certain that their return to the Víbora base was inevitable, and upon
their arrival, they would behave as though nothing had happened.
Yet, the question lingered: How long would they be gone? Or would
they all be killed? The uncertainty of their fate hung in the balance
and weighed heavily on our minds. We prayed God would protect
them. In the meantime, our battered spirits and bodies needed to
be revived and that would only happen as we spent time in God's
Word and waited (expectantly) on Him.

Out of the Mouth of Babes

For the word of God is alive and active. Sharper than any double-edged sword, it penetrates even to dividing soul and spirit, joints and marrow; it judges the thoughts and attitudes of the heart. Hebrews 4:12 NIV

During his eighteen-day hospital stay, Steve Parker seized every opportunity he could to share the Gospel among the medical staff and fellow patients. Despite all the trauma and suffering, his faith in God only grew stronger. Convinced that there was a divine purpose behind his ordeal, Steve's resolve remained unshaken. Following a recovery period of nearly seven weeks in the city, he returned to the Víbora base with his family just as he had promised.

Prior to their departure, the Parker family enjoyed a festive Christmas celebration in the city, joined by their children, including one who had flown in from the mission boarding school. The school permitted a generous month-long break for the children to spend with their families. Sammy and Becky arrived by plane to join us at the Guest Home in Cochabamba. We had a full month—four marvelous weeks, twenty-eight joyous days—to spend with our children over the holiday. The time flew by much too quickly and soon it was time to bid farewell as Sam and Becky ascended the steps of the Piper Aztec aircraft for their return flight to school. The good-byes were extremely painful for me, though I worked hard at holding back tears to spare our children the added weight of my pain. My tears would find their escape in solitude later on.

It was a common expectation at that time for missionary children to attend the mission boarding school. Our children not only received an excellent education there but also formed lasting friendships. Despite the pain of separation, I am convinced the school was crucial in shaping them into the remarkable individuals they are today. Not only are they grounded in their Christian faith but actively support missionary work along with spouses who share their Christian values. Their academic achievements give evidence to the quality of education they received at the school; all three of them excelled in their college studies. The decision to send them away was a profound sacrifice. Nevertheless, in our case, it was a divinely honored choice, made to advance the Gospel among those who might otherwise remain unreached.

I was so emotionally depleted with the aftermath of the attack and the pain of seeing our children leave, that returning to the primitive

Tambo, the mission boarding school

jungle was extremely difficult for me. Our youngest son, Caleb, was a mere five years old and was with us.

The Piper Aztec made the familiar flight over the rugged Andes, past the Yungas (rainforest foothills, or cloud-forest), and back into the deep green expanse of the Amazon rainforest, marking our return to our jungle home. The Yuquí thought they had killed Steve, leading us to anticipate a

lengthy absence before they might dare to show their faces again. Meanwhile, the Parkers had made their way back to the Víbora River base, though not without the heartache of sending their seven-year-old back to boarding school as well.

The rainforest Andean foothills

After we were settled again at the base, a lumber company reached out to our men, reporting they were having consistent contacts with what they believed were Yuquí nomads, located a mere thirty-five kilometers to our east. Communication barriers hindered their interactions with the nomads, or so they said. Would our men fly over to help? Claiming to have a 700-meter airstrip in serviceable condition, the Marabol Lumber Company invited our team to their site. With an airstrip accessible, Steve Parker, Larry Depue, and Alan boarded a small plane to fly into the area and check things out.

Upon their arrival, the landing strip presented an unexpected challenge for pilot Tom Bush and his passengers. Contrary to the company's assurances, the runway was in terrible disrepair, with trees encroaching so dangerously close, there was barely enough room for the small Cessna's wings. The approach, which should have been completely clear, was obstructed with towering trees. Alan was duly impressed with Tom's adept flying skills as he deftly tilted a wing to dodge a looming tree on approach to the airstrip.

Touching down on the overgrown airstrip, the guys wondered if they would be able to take off again without clearing it first. After taxiing to a thatch-roofed hut near the end of the runway and powering down, they learned from the caretaker that their landing was a pioneering feat; theirs was the first plane ever to land on the strip! Go figure!

Two other men with the caretaker claimed they'd had fleeting glimpses of the nomads but hadn't had any face-to-face contact with them. What was with the "consistent" contacts they had mentioned? The truth was, they were terrified of the "savages" and even more so after seeing Steve's huge scar from the recent shooting. Alan, Steve, and Larry suspected these nomads were

Steve showing his scar

from another band of Yuquí but none of them were certain.

Before taking to the air again, our guys borrowed machetes and worked their way down the center of the airstrip, clearing a swath wide enough that the propeller would not be cutting grass during the takeoff run. With Tom Bush, a seasoned jungle aviator at the helm, there was unwavering trust in his expertise. To reduce the aircraft weight, a bag containing sixty-six pounds of food and kitchenware was left behind. Plans were underway to dispatch a team to initiate outreach in the area, while also waiting for the nomads to return to our Víbora River Base.

A month passed, and just four months after the shooting incident involving Steve and Félix, the majority of our men from the Víbora base relocated to Arroyote to establish a new camp. Not only did they plan to improve the airstrip there, but also to look over the region for signs of the nomads. The team intended to start up another contact effort at that location. Meanwhile, Alan, the sole adult male back at the Víbora, together with Kerry, Steve's teenage son, assumed the responsibility of safeguarding the families and managing the base operations there.

The morning after the men's departure, Alan and I sat at the table with our youngest son to eat lunch. It happened to be Caleb's turn to say grace. With his little blond head bowed and hands folded, he voiced a heartfelt prayer, "Heavenly Father, thank you for this food, and *please* bring the nomads back *today*. Amen." His words sent a shiver down my spine. I couldn't help but wonder: What on earth made him pray the nomads would return *today?*

In my heart, I countered his prayer with a silent plea of my own, "Please Lord, don't bring them back yet. You know we aren't prepared for their return without the other men in camp." That evening, we went to bed early, sensing the void left by Sam and Becky's absence.

The following morning at the breakfast table, our youngest asked again if he could say grace. "Sure!" we said, happy to see his eagerness to pray. He bowed his little head and prayed again, with even greater fervor: "Dear Jesus, thank you for this food and *please* bring the nomads out *TODAY!*"

My pulse began to race and I lost my appetite. *WHY* was our little boy so intent on praying specifically that the nomads would return *TODAY*? Surely, the *Bia* wouldn't dare return for a lengthy time after pulling such a treacherous act on our men! Not only had they pierced Steve clear through the back with their lethal arrow, but they would have done the same to Félix if Alan had not shot his gun in the air to scare them away. As far as I was concerned, they could stay away for good! It was merely our little boy's innocent prayer, so why the panic?

As soon as we finished breakfast, I set Caleb in his room with his favorite toys, then rushed into our bedroom. Not understanding why I felt such anxiety, I threw myself on my knees next to the bed and grabbed my Bible. I needed to hear a word from God, and I needed that word ASAP! Desperate times call for desperate measures, so I did what any spiritually mature woman does in a crisis (NOT!) I opened my Bible and arbitrarily pointed to a verse. Jesus, our great Soul-ologist, understood perfectly well why that war was raging in my soul, and in His tender mercy, He spoke *very* directly to me through the verse I had so randomly pointed to. My finger had rested on Job 42:10 KJV

And the LORD turned the captivity of Job
when he prayed for his friends:

Immediately, God's Spirit made it clear to me that I was the one in captivity. Not only was I captive to my *own* will but I was seriously resisting God's will with everything in me! In truth, not only did I pray that the Yuquí would *NOT* return that day, I didn't care if I ever saw them again! I broke down before the Lord and wept. *Lord, I know I'm resisting your will but this is so hard for me.* Then I bowed my head and prayed out loud, "If it's really Your will to bring the Yuquí back *today*, help me to move out of the way. Not my will, but Yours be done."

God answered our little boy's heartfelt prayer. The Yuquí warriors returned that *very* day, the day that Alan was the only man in camp. Let me tell you all about it.

Trembling Knees

Once God made it clear to me that I had been resisting His Holy Spirit, I surrendered to His higher plan and rose with a much calmer heart to clean up the dirty dishes in the kitchen. Meanwhile, Alan was in the shed, diligently preparing additional provisions for the Arroyote team, which would be dispatched on an upcoming flight. He was focused on his task when abruptly the other women in camp frantically called out for him. There, standing at the edge of the jungle, were the very warriors who had tried to kill Steve and Félix.

Kerry, Steve's son, armed with a rifle, stayed back near the houses while Alan advanced halfway to the gift rack, staying a safe distance from the jungle. He shouted to the *Bia, "Jeguä!"* (Come).

"You come!" they responded.

"No! I am the one you can have confidence in. You come to me," Alan countered.

Potbelly, being the more expendable slave, left the safety of the woods and approached to within fifteen feet of Alan. Two Yuquí women accompanied him. Observing that neither Potbelly nor the women were harmed, Tom, Dick, Vera, Tapir, Harry, Friday, Spooky, and Whitey rallied their courage and emerged from the shadows. Ten nomads in all.

"Steve and his companions have gone to look for "your others" (the group of Yuquí roaming near the lumber camp)," Alan conveyed. "The *yatsitata* (airplane) will bring them back here tomorrow; until then, no bananas will be given to you."

Watching my husband intently, Tom asked. "Why are your legs trembling?"

"Your legs would be trembling too if your friends shot you like you did to us!" Alan retorted. While he tried to remain calm, he couldn't keep his legs from shaking.

"The young man behind me holding a gun is Steve's son. He has orders to shoot you in the legs if you touch me in any way. *Papaguasu* (Big Father—God) watched over Steve and made him well again. Steve will show himself to you tomorrow and he will give you the bananas." With the promise of bananas, the nomads retreated back into the jungle depths. Alan hastily got on the radio to arrange for a plane to retrieve Steve and the other men.

The following morning, heavy rain pelted our tin roof. My husband listened to the beating of the rain as he lay in the hammock, convinced the nomads wouldn't show up in such terrible weather. Abruptly, Steve's voice broke through his thoughts. "We have visitors out by the rack."

Prior to this, it had been agreed that Steve would not be armed with a gun to avoid giving the impression he wanted revenge. On the other hand, the rest of the men were armed with either revolvers or rifles. Even though our men carried guns, the *Bia* didn't hesitate to come right into our camp. Without any prompting from the team, they left their bows and arrows behind. Soon, everyone was sitting around a warm fire under the shelter where we normally visited with them. Sweetened rice was prepared, and bananas were offered to the thirteen visiting nomads.

The missionaries laid out strict requirements before we would

Some happy porkers eating plantains

resume normal relations with them again. When they asked to have their tools sharpened, Alan let the *Bia* know that none of their tools would be sharpened until Steve's pack, the machetes, mosquito nets, and all the other items they had stolen were returned. As the rain lightened, the nomads wanted to see Alan's growing piglets hoping they would be gifted with one. However, it was emphasized once again: *no* piglets would be distributed until *all* stolen items were returned.

As the visit continued, it was evident that they still posed a threat to us. When Alan suggested, "Move your camp close to us so we can see you more often and feed you," they responded, "Come to our camp to prove that we have moved in close and then we will return your stolen items."

That afternoon, Alan reached out to Bob Garland via radio at the Chimoré River base. "Bob, can you get Straight Hair and Wooly Hair to come over to help us? We're in urgent need of their assistance." Our Yuquí coworkers would understand their nomadic kin and have a better feel for what the warriors were thinking.

However, it would be three more months before the hostile group reappeared. Nightly downpours led to repeated flooding at our base, making it impossible for the nomads to come back given the swollen waters. They likely retreated to the higher jungle terrain across the Chore River until the flood waters subsided.

As the flood receded and the camp dried out, the team's optimism for their return also grew. One day, while working in his shed, Alan shouted toward the house, "Vickie, check if there are any nomads near the gift rack." He suspected he had heard a faint hoot from that area.

"I don't see any nomads from here," I responded. Felix also thought he'd heard a distant hoot and joining Alan, the two ventured to the jungle's edge. Approaching, they noticed Steve's backpack hanging on the gift rack. Moments later, the nomads emerged from the shadows.

Alan greeted them and after interacting with them, began inquiring about the other items they had stolen. They didn't return those articles spontaneously but only after each item was specifically requested.

Once the *Bia* left for the day and a flight delivered Straight Hair, Wooly Hair and their wives from the Chimoré base to the Víbora River base, the team felt better prepared to interact with the nomads. That night, a cold rainstorm blew in from the south, so we had no visitors for the next three days. When they did show up again, the nomads returned with most of the items our men had requested; thus, the relationship with them was restored to a degree, but some major changes needed to be put in place first.

Steve would now manage all the trade goods, requiring the nomads to approach him for their needs. We hoped this would foster respect for him and lead to an apology for their past treachery. When they wanted to go fishing in the boat with the team, our men carried firearms but prohibited the warriors from carrying their weapons, sending clear signals of our distrust.

Alan and our Yuquí brothers from the Chimoré addressed the warriors with stern gravity about their assault, making it unmistakably clear that any further malicious actions would *NOT* be tolerated. In the beginning, the warriors had appeared somewhat flippant about shooting our men. Life was cheap to them. Once they saw how resolute the team was and that our men meant business, their attitudes took on a much more serious note.

The *Bia* resumed their regular visits to our camp, but I remained inside our jungle home. Knowing our furlough (home assignment to the U.S.) was just around the corner, I determined not to interact with the *Bia* before we left. I wasn't ready to face them again.

Some of These Are Mine

The nomads showed up one more time before we left for our home assignment in the U.S. I stayed inside our jungle house, peering through our screened window to observe the other missionaries as they interacted with them. Alan was walking toward the pig pen with a group of nomads trailing behind.

Alan's hogs never ceased to delight the nomads and it amused them watching him interact with his tame and well cared for pigs. Later, the *Bia* followed another colleague to the hut where gifts were stored. Several pieces of bright red fabric were given to them, a gift they really treasured.

Though I harbored no resentment toward them, especially considering their deeply lost condition both physically and spiritually, I couldn't bring myself to face the *Bia* again. I didn't realize it at the time, but I was going through severe culture shock with a strong case of PTSD thrown in. The sun was setting behind the

Sun setting over jungle river

darkening jungle trees, and the nomads had begun their departure.

Banana-laden palm leaf bundles cascaded down their backs, secured by sturdy vines encircling their brows as they filed across the clearing to the jungle's edge.

The forest canopy was bathed in a deep emerald green at that time of evening and the atmosphere almost shivered with the shrill serenade of cicadas. My gaze was held captive by the procession of cinnamon-colored figures traversing the clearing before melding into the forest's embrace, the bright red fabric draped over their shoulders highlighting the rich tones of their golden-brown skin. Armed with formidable bow and arrows, the warriors led the way, followed by male and female slaves burdened beneath the weight of their loads. In a single file, they vanished—one by one—into the verdant green rainforest, each soul a fleeting shadow in the mysterious depths of the jungle.

I was entirely absorbed by the profound beauty of the scene and regretted not having a camera ready to capture its essence. The scenario was so poignant, so profoundly rich and moving. Abruptly, a question interrupted my musings, posing a heart-wrenching question for me: *To what lengths would you go to rescue these human souls if one of them was your own child?*

I was stunned by the query. *My own child! I would do ANYTHING to save my children from such a wretched life and my resolve would be absolutely unwavering! Regardless of the sacrifices, I would not give up until each one of them was safely home.* Just the drive to alleviate my child's physical sufferings from the dangerous and inhospitable jungle was compelling enough.

The inquiry deepened, probing the very depths of my soul. *What about securing them for eternity?* The question forced me to weigh the gravity of the nomads' plight against eternal separation from God, separation from their Creator's love and goodness forever! The devil's malevolent forces were making every effort to deceive the nomads and bring them with him into that endless abyss that awaited him and his demons. My willingness to do anything for my child stood in stark contrast to the unwillingness I felt about continuing our efforts with the nomads. Tears streamed down my face. We missionaries were the only link between the vanishing Yuquí and the wonderful news of the Gospel. We represented their sole connection to hope, enlightenment, and the redemptive power of Jesus Christ.

As my eyes lingered on the encroaching twilight of the jungle bordering our open space, a gentle, yet distinct inner voice emerged once again. *Some of these Yuquí nomads will respond to the Gospel and become my own children.*

> *But as many as received Him, to them He gave the*
> *right to become children of God, John 1:12 NKJV*

There was a long silence as I pondered the profound suffering that God's own Son endured on the cross to save humanity from sin, death, and eternal darkness in hell. Only God's unfathomable love for these small groups of vanishing nomads could have compelled us to persevere in spite of all the obstacles, suffering, and hardships we faced. Only Jesus!

> *What man of you, having a hundred sheep, if he*
> *loses one of them, does not leave the ninety-nine...*
> *and go after the one which is lost until he*
> *finds it? And when he has found it, he lays it on*
> *his shoulders, rejoicing. Luke 15: 4–5 NKJV*

> *...And they shall be **mine**, says the LORD of hosts,*
> *on that day when I make up my jewels; and*
> *I will spare them, as a man spares his own son*
> *that serves him. Malachi 3:17 KJV*

Father and son

Chief and Favorite Joven

Potbelly's Escape

The *Bia* were gone on their nomadic wanderings for another three months. During their absence, our mission boarding school celebrated its end of year commemorations and programs, a joyous occasion for both students and families. With our impending departure to the U.S. for home assignment, we chose not to return to the jungle after the festivities.

During our leave in the homeland, our Yuquí colleagues assisted our fellow missionaries in encouraging the nomadic Yuquí to settle down at the Chimoré base. We hoped to bring together the nomads with their relatives who were already settled, creating a lasting and stable community within the supportive setting of the jungle base.

A falling out had emerged among the nomads at that time, particularly between Tom and Dick, the two young brothers leading the band of twenty-four. Dick, along with the *Bia* who supported him, returned to our Víbora base. Once again, the invitation was extended to visit the big farm where they could meet more of their Yuquí relatives. After some negotiation and the incentive of returning with sugarcane and treats, Dick and his slave Potbelly, agreed to brave the flight. Potbelly displayed more courage than Dick, who remained hunkered down on the aircraft floor throughout the fifteen-minute flight.

By that time, our family had settled in Spokane, Washington, where we spent the first six months of home assignment. We received regular updates by amateur radio from our coworkers at the Víbora jungle base. Larry Depue was able to make "phone patches" through a radio operator in the United States to keep us abreast of the jungle dwellers' situation. The nomads' plight weighed heavily upon our hearts, and we prayed daily for them as well as for our coworkers who continued with the outreach.

About five months into our time in Spokane, as we were tucked into our beds one night, I was having trouble falling asleep, so I quietly made my way up the stairs to the living room. Sitting in a chair, I picked up a small photograph album lying on the coffee table. As I sifted through images of the *Bia*, I was struck by a particularly distressing photo of Potbelly. His gaunt appearance and vacant gaze conveyed a profound sense of loss.

Potbelly, the abused slave

As I looked at his picture, a heavy and penetrating burden to pray for this slave came over me. I pleaded with God to make a way for Potbelly to join his kin at the Chimoré Base, knowing that there he would be provided with nourishing food and receive the medical attention he needed. There, he would be treated with respect and humanity rather than as a mere animal. The angst and burden for this lowly Yuquí man did not lift from my heart for another ten minutes or more and seemed to come over me in waves of intensity. I can only equate it to spiritual labor pains taking place deep within my soul. Then, just like that, the burden lifted. Being quite late, I made my way back downstairs to bed.

Early the next morning, the telephone shattered the stillness with a shrill ring. I answered the phone.

"Will you accept a collect call from Larry?" said an unfamiliar voice on the other end.

I was confused for a moment and then realized the caller was referring to Larry Depue, our coworker at the Víbora jungle base.

The call was being relayed to us through an amateur radio operator Stateside.

Larry's voice was brimming with excitement as he related to us the most recent happenings at the Víbora camp. After a three-month absence, the nomads had finally returned. The night before, the exact night I was praying for him, Potbelly had made a life altering decision: to sneak away from his people and return to the missionary camp alone. The *Bia* had taken away his wife and the abuse he faced was so extreme, the missionaries feared for his life. Having previously visited the Chimoré base, he begged the missionaries to relocate him to join his relatives at the big farm.

The next day, Potbelly was transported to the Chimoré where he received the loving care he needed. What an amazing and truly remarkable answer to my prayers! It was evident that divine intervention was clearly at play, orchestrating events unbeknownst to us; the timing could not have been more perfect. What a privilege it was to share in God's divine concern for this lowly, abused slave simply by praying for him. Oh, the glorious power there is in prayer offered by those who have placed their faith in God's Son!

A week after Potbelly's transfer, the nomads revisited the Víbora base. Initially, Dick and the others were angry over his slave's escape and subsequent aid from the missionaries. Thanks to the peacemaking efforts of our Yuquí comrades from the Chimoré base, the nomads departed on friendly terms. Two months later, we were informed of further developments through a letter from Steve and Vangie Parker, albeit with some alterations for clarity:

A distant hoot broke the quietness of the morning. "Vangie, check the gift rack!" Steve alerted her.

"Nobody is there," his wife replied.

Then they heard it: another hoot coming from the edge of the clearing. They ran outside to get a better view and noticed several nomads hiding behind a tree. After waiting for more than eight weeks for the *Bia* to return, the missionaries were overjoyed to see them. Previously, the team had decided that during the next contact, they would bring Potbelly, the slave who deserted his band, over to the Víbora base with some of the Yuquí believers. They hoped this would encourage the nomads to join them at the big farm.

Once the *Bia* came out from hiding and settled in camp next to a big pot of boiling rice, the missionaries made arrangements for a flight to bring over a much more robust Potbelly, Bob Garland, and some Yuquí believers from the Chimoré base.

Upon their arrival, the groups engaged in earnest dialogue with one another. The *Bia* made promises about visiting the faraway farm, but after two hours, decided to leave. Our coworkers followed the nomads to the edge of the jungle, pleading with them to stay. It seemed one warrior was inclined to do so but was dissuaded by his spouse. The band then trailed into the shadowy depths of the rainforest without looking back. Broken hearted, our coworkers returned to their houses feeling the heavy weight of the nomads' decision.

Two hours later as dusk approached, a missionary radioing the Chimoré base conveyed the sad message: "Even after witnessing Potbelly's health and wellbeing, they've turned down our proposals to relocate them to the Chimoré. Their refusal was heartbreaking." He was just about to continue when he was abruptly halted. From outside, he heard joyous and jubilant cries signaling new hope. "They've returned, and they've brought their hammocks and families with them!" With elation, the missionaries ran out to meet their jungle friends with open arms.

The *Bia* asked to spend the night at the Víbora before heading to the Chimoré base the following day. Brimming with joy, our colleagues thanked and praised God again and again. Once the nomads set up camp, the missionaries took them hunting and the Lord provided plenty of meat for them to roast over their fires that night. The following morning, the nomads were gifted with blankets and other essentials as the missionaries saw them off on the first of several flights to the Chimoré camp.

Steve recounted, "As the last group of nomads departed to reunite with their relatives at the Chimoré, we reflected over the final seven years of our missionary work filled with so much sacrifice and suffering... always hoping, praying, and believing God would reach them. Then we noticed a vibrant arc, a brilliant rainbow stretching clear across the sky, as though God was reminding us of His faithful commitment to fulfill His promises. As we go forth to reach a lost world for Jesus's sake, He goes with us every step of the way."

The burden on God's heart to save these hopeless wanderers infinitely surpassed our own. His crucifixion is an eternal testament to the lengths Jesus Christ will go to rescue the human race from an eternity of anguish and darkness; the height to which He yearns to raise those who place their faith in Him is clearly manifested in His resurrection. What about you? Have you received His free gift of salvation? You will be left with an eternity of regret if you reject Him.

Within a year after the nomads from the Víbora River area settled at the Chimoré base, a third small band of Yuquí was also befriended and moved to join their kinfolk; but as we, the Fosters, had no hand in that, someone else will have to tell that story.

Thirty years of sacrificial missionary effort were required to preserve fewer than ninety Yuquí from annihilation by the encroaching world. Was it worth all the investment of time, money, and the physical and mental trauma on the part of the missionary team?

★★★★★★★

Epilogue

To what can I compare our missionary quest of reaching the Yuquí nomads? Searching for hidden treasure? This small band was certainly *hidden*, shrouded beneath the vast canopy of the Amazonian rainforest. Trying to locate them was more like trying to find a needle in a haystack, only these needles kept on the move. No, searching for hidden treasure isn't an adequate comparison.

Rivers winding through Amazonian jungle

How about searching for extremely rare and precious jewels found only in one particular place on planet earth? There's no doubt that this small people-group was *rare* indeed; very few groups of only about thirty Yuquí each wandered through the vast Amazon jungle. Precious? The nationals certainly didn't think so. These "primitive" and dangerous jungle warriors were despised by the nationals who recognized the Bia as nothing but "brute savages." The Bolivian government was preparing to send in the military to completely annihilate the Yuquí. No, searching for rare and precious jewels isn't a satisfactory analogy either.

I've got it! Our missionary quest was more like searching for children trapped under the rubbish of a collapsed building. Yes, that's more like it! These aren't just any children though. These are your *very own*; and without human intervention, they will perish. Can you sense the urgency? Can you comprehend the pain you'd be willing to endure to save your precious children? Progress may have been made and your hopes soared as you heard the children's cries beneath the debris; but then, more rubble fell and muffled their screams. You are at the point of exhaustion! Your body has deep wounds from the exertion and you hurt all over.

At this point, you might throw your hands up in the air and declare, "Oh well! At least we gave it a good try! No! Never! Maybe you'd give up the quest for jewels or hidden treasures; those are just material things. But give up on human beings, especially when they are your own beloved children? Never! You would give and give and keep on giving. That, dear reader, is a fitting analogy of our missionary quest. However, these children were not our own; they were God's. Knowing that some of these treacherous nomads would embrace His Son and the Gospel message, He relentlessly pursued them.

This book is not so much my story as it is a testament to the boundless measures Christ will undertake to seek and save the lost. My journey was simply in sync with His guidance, seeking His direction for my life. Unbeknownst to me, this alignment with Jesus's teachings and my commitment to Him as a "jungle bride" enriched my life far beyond measure, not only in my existence on earth, but for all eternity.

> *O the deep, deep love of Jesus,*
> *Vast, unmeasured, boundless, free,*
> *Rolling as a mighty ocean*
> *In its fullness over me.*
> *Underneath me, all around me,*
> *Is the current of Thy love;*
> *Leading onward, leading homeward*
> *To Thy glorious rest above.*
> *(Hymn by S. Trevor Francis)*

About the Author

The author's journey during the creation of 'Jungle Bride' was marked by profound challenges, reflecting a deep commitment to befriend hostile jungle nomads and preserving them from certain annihilation. Encroachment by loggers and farmers threatened the Yuquí's ancestral lands. Despite the perils faced, including the wounding of six colleagues by the Yuquí's formidable arrows, Vickie and her husband Alan were driven by a God-given passion to learn the unique culture and language of these nomads and introduce them to the loving Creator God who longed to rescue them from destruction. Witnessing the Yuquí's survival, addressing their health needs, and conveying the compassionate love of God made the sacrifices involved worth it all. Vickie and Alan retired in 2018 after forty-eight years of missionary work and now reside in Green Valley, Arizona.

Printed in the United States
by Baker & Taylor Publisher Services